PENGUIN BOOKS

THE SECRET LIFE OF CAT OWNERS

Bruce Fogle DVM, MRCVS runs a veterinary practice in London and lectures on animal behaviour at veterinary colleges internationally. He has written a number of books on pet care and the behavioural problems of pets, including *The Cat's Mind* and *The Dog's Mind*, *101 Questions Your Cat Would Ask Its Vet* and *101 Questions Your Dog Would Ask Its Vet*, and a companion volume to this book, *The Secret Life of Dog Owners*. He is the world's best-selling practising vet.

BRUCE FOGLE DVM, MRCVS

THE SECRET LIFE
OF CAT OWNERS

PENGUIN BOOKS

PENGUIN BOOKS

Published by the Penguin Group
Penguin Books Ltd, 27 Wrights Lane, London W8 5TZ, England
Penguin Putnam Inc., 375 Hudson Street, New York, New York 10014, USA
Penguin Books Australia Ltd, Ringwood, Victoria, Australia
Penguin Books Canada Ltd, 10 Alcorn Avenue, Toronto, Ontario, Canada M4V 3B2
Penguin Books (NZ) Ltd, 182–190 Wairau Road, Auckland 10, New Zealand

Penguin Books Ltd, Registered Offices: Harmondsworth, Middlesex, England

First published by Pelham 1997
Published in Penguin Books 1998
3 5 7 9 10 8 6 4 2

CONTENTS

Of course the idea is silly. Cats are interested in themselves, not in what drives the people in their lives to do what they do. A decent cat wants security, comfort and a conveyor belt of fresh food without having to work too hard for any of these luxuries. It wants periodic excitement interspersed with long lulls of cozy inactivity. Your cat doesn't give two hoots about why you behave with him or her the way you do.

But if you've got this far you can count yourself among cat owners who genuinely care about their cats. And I'm speaking as a veterinarian. Over a quarter of a century ago, when I started practising clinical veterinary medicine, cats were 'just there'. Dogs made up over ninety per cent of my patients. Cats were expendable. Today in the United States, Canada, Britain and elsewhere, there are more pet cats than pet dogs. The cat has become our favourite animal companion. New breeds and colours appear yearly.

For the first time in the history of cats we are actively intervening in their breeding, intentionally producing dwarfed breeds with deformed legs, or hairless breeds with skin wrinkles. We pass legislation restricting cats to leads or enforcing their return to their own homes from sunset to sunrise. We confine them for their entire lives to an indoor existence. Why do we behave this way? It would be quite a unique cat that might ask this type of question but I also know that genuine cat lovers are conscientious enough to want to understand their own motives in keeping cats.

During the last fifteen years, social, behavioural and biological scientists around the world have investigated our relationship with cats and have published fascinating results. The answers to many of the questions that follow are based upon their thoughts or their statistics. It seems that the reasons we are happy to live with the world's most efficient small land-predator are more complicated and more interesting than we once thought.

CHAPTER ONE

The Secret Instincts of Cat Owners

1. *A simple question: I purr, I meow, I hiss. I even chirp. Exactly how good are people at understanding what I'm saying?*

Pretty good. Certainly at getting the gist of the message, although they are not as good at the subtleties of cat talk.

Cat sounds fall into three distinct categories: high-pitched warning noises, lower, softer murmuring sounds and just plain cat talk. People are quite good at understanding warning noises – hissing and spitting in particular. To hiss, a cat opens its mouth about halfway, curls its tongue into an open-topped tube and expels a jet of hot, angry air from its lungs. People have an instinctive antipathy towards snakes and the cat's hiss is a clever method of mimicking a snake's warning signal. The meaning of spitting is just as easy to understand. After all, some people still unwittingly resort to this behaviour when they are angry.

People are quite good at interpreting appealing murmuring sounds too. They instinctively identify purring and chirping, the cat's two most common murmurs, as sounds of content-ment, pleasure and relaxation. But some people forget that cats also purr to calm themselves down when they are frightened, anxious or even in pain. People get these sounds right because here, too, people have similar sounds of relaxation and con-tentment; moans and sighs.

They are not as good understanding cat talk. Talk always contains vowel sounds. Cats understand the differences in in-flection between 'miaowwww', 'miiiiaow' and 'miaaaaow' but, curiously, people have to learn these differences. Of course cats know that 'miaowwww' means 'feed me instantly', 'miiiiaow means' 'my litter tray is a disgrace' and 'miaaaaow' means 'I need human contact now'. But people do not instinctively understand. They need training, not just from any cat, but from the speaker itself. That is because unlike human languages, each of which is spoken by many people in similar ways, cat language varies from cat to cat. Each cat pronounces its vowels uniquely, in its own idiosyncratic fashion. With training, observant people quickly learn the individual vowel sounds, the distinctive voice, of their own cat.

2. *But how good are people at understanding what I do?*

People and cats do a number of similar things: both are heat seeking comfort lovers, naturally inclined to drop whatever they are doing if a shaft of sunlight enters their lives; both like to rest frequently, indeed people know that their behaviour is so similar to that of cats they call it 'catnapping'; when given the opportunity, both like to snack on food, nibbling throughout the day; both prefer to use a specific site for going to the toilet; many people even share the cat's predisposition to slumber all day and party all night. People's instincts are moderately good at understanding what cats do because often their objectives are similar.

In other areas, people fail miserably to understand what cats do and why they do it. They think that when their cat scratches furniture and climbs curtains it does so primarily to annoy people. They think that spraying urine on the walls or urinating in sinks is a cat's way of making statements to owners. They think that missing the litter tray is done to get even, and that not burying droppings is a sign of lack of hygiene, rather than a symbol of authority that any other cat instantly recognizes and understands.

People think that cats behave in certain ways to 'get even' because getting even is such a potent need in people's own lives. There is no doubt that retribution is part of a cat's behavioural repertoire but this cat characteristic is much less important to cats than to people. In a nutshell, because people are pack animals and cats are not, people often misinterpret what cats do.

3. *Okay. Then how good are they at understanding what I need?*

Now here we have a problem. Many people think that if all the outward necessities of human existence are offered to a cat, its needs are met. Conscientious cat owners provide tasty, nutritious food, warm, safe and secure accommodation and companionship. Then they complain to their vet that the cat steals food from the table, leaves home for days at a time and scratches them when it is petted.

People mistakenly translate human needs directly into similar feline necessities but these do not always equate. After all, cats are still, in the depths of their souls, solitary hunters rather than opportunist scavengers. They are currently in the process of a natural evolution from hunter to scavenger but the hunting instinct, the biological need to seek out, capture and kill, remains supreme. People often forget that cats get as much pleasure out of finding their own food as they can get from eating it. It is a supreme thrill for a cat to scent a meal, scale the heights of counter tops and discover succulent food.

People enjoy the constancy and security of their own homes. They feel relaxed and comfortable in them. They feel upset, let down, even emotionally abused when a cat turns its back on its home and what people consider to be the cat's family, and goes off wandering. They feel they are failures if their cat finds another house nearby more to its liking and settles in there. People fail to understand that many cats attach themselves to territory, not to people, and are happy to disengage from that territory if another is more alluring.

People thrive on intimacy, they enjoy hearing words of comfort and need routine physical contact with other people. They usually think that cats need intimacy too, but they don't. Cats are not interested in holding hands. Cats evolved as loners and are not as dependent as people are. Each follows its own personal path through life. Through selective breeding, people have intentionally attempted to reduce the cat's supreme autonomy. The dependent kitten in all cats – playfulness and enjoyment in physical contact with others – has been enhanced. But the cat's actual need for human touch is not nearly as profound as that of the people it lives with.

4. *I feel safer with women than men. Why is it that women are more likely to devote their lives to my welfare?*

Probably because women are simply a lot nicer than men: after all, which sex is responsible for most car accidents, for most assaults, for most burglaries, for most murders?

Sociologists constantly try to prove that humans are uniquely different from all other mammals, that fathers can 'mother' as well as mothers can. They cannot. Human genetics and human hormones make women more natural care givers than men. Men bring their own values to the care of their children and unknowingly apply these same values to their relationships with their cats. A human father's role involves stimulating his children; he naturally winds them up, and plays rough-and-tumble games with them. Fathers don't take their sons to sports matches simply as a cultural phenomenon. It is in men's genetic and hormonal make-up to combat for food or for supremacy, which is why men are not as concerned as women are when cats kill birds. Men instinctively understand the cat's need to hunt (I know one man who takes his Siamese cat with him when he goes hunting, and relishes his cat's inclination to climb into trees and leap on the backs of passing cattle). It also means that men are more likely to be callous with cats, to abuse them, and even to kill them.

Just as with all other primates, women are biologically better care givers than men: they comfort; they nurture; they nurse. And they do so their entire lives. Even if they have their own human families, some women have such a surfeit of warmth and generosity in them that they devote themselves to the welfare of other animals. Some of these women do so because they find it difficult to form deep emotional bonds with fellow humans, but the majority are simply following their biological instincts. That is why well over three quarters of all members of animal welfare organizations are women. It is also why women fill a similar membership percentage of vegetarian groups.

5. *It seems that men prefer dogs to cats. Why exactly do I appeal to women more than men?*

Instinct once again. For whatever the reason may be, and that includes how their brains are 'pre-wired', or how sex hormone influences a man's brain from before he is born, men and women have different attitudes to animals. At its most simple, women are better at recognizing human facial expressions and body language than men. They are probably better at understanding feline expressions and body language too. Certainly, in clinical veterinary medicine, I have observed that women know when something is wrong with their pets earlier than men do.

By looking at the different ways in which men and women approach parenting you also get a clue about their orientation towards cats. When a contented mother sees her baby she softens her tone and starts to speak in high pitched 'motherese'. 'Hello darling' she ululates in a pitch higher than her natural one. As she speaks she gently touches her baby's feet or hands. Then, still smiling and talking in a distinctive language she uses only for children, she moves her hands softly up her baby's arms or legs until they reach the torso. All the time she keeps her eyes on her baby's big eyes. Listen to women talking to their cats and you hear the same language, high pitched words often with question marks: 'Fluffy want din dins? Mummy's here'. Cats release a woman's latent and everlasting need to nurture.

Men instinctively need to nurture too but they do so in different ways. When a relaxed father meets his baby he does not lapse into 'motherese' as seventy per cent of mothers do. Most fathers, in fact a similar seventy per cent, continue to speak in their natural voice, only slowing down their words. 'Hi kid. What's up?', Dad says as he touches his baby's torso rather than its extremities, often with a gentle jab rather than a soft caress. This is a greeting that dogs quite like but cats find less amusing.

A man's manifestation of attachment includes behaviour that a more sociably gregarious species like the dog is drawn to. Cats find this behaviour rather crude and unsophisticated. One consequence is that men soon learn that dogs respond to them in ways they understand and enjoy. Dogs are physical. Cats are ethereal. Men, more instinctively addicted to nature than nurture, are drawn to dogs.

Size, however, is the ultimate consideration. Domestic cats are the size of newborn babies, the most potent releaser of maternal instincts. Men who have no interest in domestic cats, who feel that association with kitty impunes their masculinity, are instinctively drawn to the big cats; pumas, lions, tigers, jaguars. Man the hunter is quite happy to bask in the glory of the superior abilities of the big feline hunter.

6. *I'm the most successful land based killer on the planet. Why do advertisers always think of me as feminine?*

Because advertisers understand human instincts better than the most worthy academics. Advertisers know that, like music, animals in ads are 'non denominational'. They know that animals stimulate hearts and minds and that people's responses to these animals are independent of age, sex and social class. Animals hold people's attention and they can suggest fidelity, strength, endurance, sensuality, sexuality, faithfulness, sympathy and continuity.

Different species have different meanings. The horse in beer and cigarette ads is a symbol of freedom and masculinity. It would be ridiculous to state verbally in a commercial that if you smoke this or drink that you will be more potent, but this is fine as a subliminal value of the product when portrayed through the behaviour of a horse.

Cats have particular 'female' qualities. They are small, soft, warm, child-like, and elegant. In our culture they symbolize the indoors rather than outdoors. All of these qualities activate and focus the mind; they get the viewer's or reader's attention and stimulate emotions. (Dog's on the other hand, have male values. Dogs are strong, fast, companionable and symbolize the outdoors.)

In one study, an international detergent maker made seven different advertisements for their product and investigated how many people remembered the product seven days after seeing them. Thirty-two per cent recalled the name of the product when it featured a next-door-neighbour type of woman, thirty-eight per cent when it featured a bird, forty-eight per cent when a famous person promoted the product, sixty-two per cent when a horse was involved, seventy-one per cent for a chimpanzee, seventy-seven per cent when a dog was in the commercial and eighty-two per cent when a cat was the main image.

Advertisers use pets for different reasons: pets don't grow old – the dog or cat is an eternal Peter Pan, never ageing; pets look beautiful; they are spontaneous and truthful; pets don't lie. In advertising, animals act as similes and metaphors for products. Rather than appearing to be the supremely efficient killer that it really is, the cat in commercials is a totem of our past. It stirs images and meanings lost in our distant memory and acts in ways humans can't. All the typical feline qualities are thought of as feminine, which is why to advertisers the cat is such a superb metaphor.

7. *I was taught to look but not touch. In fact, in the natural world I only touch my own kind when I fight, have sex or if they are really close relatives. Why do people always want to touch, not just look?*

People, unlike cats, instinctively need to touch. If they are starved of human contact they wither emotionally and physically.

Touch is the first and perhaps most important of all human senses. As a child grows the sensation of touching mother is relived through touching other items that psychologists call 'transitional objects'; the satin edge of a blanket and the soft, furry teddy bear. Even in adulthood people relive that feeling of security and comfort when they stroke their cat's warm, soft, silky body. This is why a cat owner's blood pressure drops when she strokes her cat. Her state of arousal is diminished because she is re-enacting the lost feeling of contentment she enjoyed at her mother's breast. Strange isn't it?

Cats are different; kittens suckle for six weeks for nourishment, then another six weeks for emotional reward and that is the end of their period of profound physical contact with others. For the next few months a kitten plays with its litter mates, but play becomes increasingly vicious, especially between males or between males and females, until this form of physical contact ceases. When food is limited, cats no longer have any contact at all with each other except when mating and even then the female is likely to turn and bite the male. When food is unlimited, female cats will live together but only seldom touch each other. Touch is limited to care of the young; either their own or kittens of close relatives.

Touching others is unimportant for cats but a primary need

for primates like people. People hunger for physical contact, it is more important even than words. They fail to understand that their craving is not universally shared by the rest of the animal world.

8. *Is that also why people gaze at me in such an intimidating way?*

People are unaware that they find it easier to look into a strange cat's eyes than they do to look into a strange person's eyes, and are often equally unaware that their unblinking stare is a sign of intimidating dominance.

Infants stare, but by the time they reach school age both their instincts and their experience have taught them to avert their eyes. Staring is one of the most powerful but unapparent behaviours that people exhibit.

In adulthood, frank staring is frowned upon. Gaze is regulated, even within families. Only the most dominant people are permitted to stare. This instinctive behaviour has existed in virtually all cultures and was perpetuated in ritual form into modern times in some countries where commoners were not allowed to look upon their king.

Instinct and learning regulate how long people may stare at other people, but staring is rewarding. That is why films and television are so popular; viewers can gaze as long as they want. That is also why the surrounding environment is so appealing – by shifting their attention outward from themselves, by watching and listening, people lower their state of arousal. Nature encourages unlimited looking and cats are part of nature. Cats virtually invite people to gaze upon them and when people do they feel more relaxed. In human relations this is a personal freedom limited by instinctive and cultural constraints.

9. *I'm not complaining, I'm just curious: why am I allowed to sleep in my owner's bedroom but their very own human children are not?*

Part of the answer is sex. Affluent middle-class couples enjoy having the privacy of their own bedrooms in which to do what they want to do. They don't want little Michael or Catherine popping up to ask what's happening. Cats, on the other hand, ask no questions. Usually, they sleep through any nocturnal human gymnastics although some cats get annoyed at humans interrupting their sleep and, with apparent disgust, leave the bedroom.

Cats are allowed in bedrooms, even during times of human intimacy, for curious but in part instinctive reasons. First of all, cats are seen as non-judgemental. The cat sees no evil, hears no evil and does not spread gossip. It is a reliable voyeur. Equally, some human senses are not as refined as those of other animals. In the survival of the fittest, people have come to rely upon the hearing, scenting and night vision of other animals. The presence of a cat in the bedroom gives an instinctive feeling of security, at least from the presence of rats and mice.

10. *Do people really think I understand what they say?*

Clark Gable, of all people, once said 'The test of a beautiful friendship is when you reach home you know that on the other side of the doorstep somebody is listening.' It is not as important, in people's minds, that cats understand what they say; it is more important to people simply that they are there.

In the deepest human friendships people sit silently for hours in each other's company and feel better for doing so. In the most profound silence people can offer each other social support. Mysteriously, just by being together, people know they are loved, cared for and valued. Mutely, in a primitive, non-verbal way, people communicate with each other through looks and touches. Expressions of affection, concern, care and love are given without the need for words. The cat's muteness is uncomplicated. Its silence says more than words, which complicate relationships. People think their cats understand every word because they communicate on such a profoundly instinctive basis. Such is the relationship that many people have with their cats.

11. *I don't talk, I just stare. So why do they think I understand their moods?*

Once again, this is a 'helpless' instinctive response on the part of humans.

People use verbal language to communicate but there are other, more basic, forms of communication such as body language and even scent, that they share with other mammals, including cats. The language instinct just happens to be the human's unique way of passing information from one to another. Using his language instinct in the most thrillingly articulate manner, the cognitive scientist Steven Pinker, in *The Language Instinct* says, 'Language is no more a cultural invention than is upright posture. Though language is a magnificent ability unique to *Homo sapiens* among living species, it does not call for sequestering the study of humans from the domain of biology, for magnificent abilities unique to particular species are far from unique in the animal kingdom. We are simply a species of primate with our own act in nature's talent show, a knack for communicating information about who did what to whom by modulating the sounds we make when we exhale.'

Humans use their own set of references to understand the world around them. In their evolution they have come to understand, as have all other mammals, that the quiet and solitude of other animals is a symbol of safety and security, and that disquiet and agitation are signs of impending danger. Humans, a gregariously sociable species, enjoy the companionship of other humans. Just being in their presence is comforting. In the deepest of relationships they know that simply by being relaxed and content in each other's company they understand each other's needs. So it is with cat company; people feel that if their cat comes into the room and restfully and contentedly settles down, it understands the needs and emotions of the person.

12. *If I'm so soft and feminine and cuddly and nice why am I used for target practice?*

Cat owners seldom use their own cats for target practice. Others do. Cats may be sensuous and baby-like to their owners, but to others they can be vermin or simply part of rampant nature, to be controlled and subdued by the most dominant species in the world.

Even cat owners can be lethally dangerous to cats they don't know. At its root, people's ambivalence towards cats has its foundations in cultural ethics. An interesting parallel is found in breeding units for laboratory mice. At the very best breeding facilities, the captive mice live in mouse heaven: they receive the tastiest and most nutritious food; they are kept free from infectious disease; mouse behaviourists devise strategies and games for the mice to play so that they do not become bored; they are allowed to breed and care for their young. All that can be done is done to ensure the emotional and physical wellbeing of these mice.

But in these laboratory-mouse breeding facilities also live unwanted mice, mice that are not part of the breeding pro-gramme. They are not under human control and are ruthlessly exterminated with traps and poison. They are not, however, much different from the captive mice. In fact they are descend-ants of captives that have escaped and now live outside the controlled colony. Under one set of conditions we value one mouse while under another set of conditions we strive to kill its brother.

It is the same with cats. If a cat is under human control it is safer than if it is independent, but even dependent cats are at risk and that is because of their small size. People kick cats because people are bullies and know they are stronger than cats. They don't kick bears or hyenas or gorillas because it is too risky. Cats are abused for much the same reason that children are abused, often by the same people. People who have been dumped on by life dump on those that are least likely to be able to defend themselves.

13. *Why are little boys so mean and little girls so boring?*

It is true. Girls are likely to mother cats, smother them with affection; a behaviour that cats will, at best, reluctantly accept. Girls use kittens and cats as learning models for parenting. As a veterinarian I sometimes see unexpected consequences, such as gangrenous legs caused by elastic bands used to keep clothing on. Girls are likely to treat pet cats the way they treat other transitional child substitutes like dolls.

Boys may be gentle, caring and considerate to their cats but at some time around puberty, even the most pleasant of boys may indulge in unpleasant, even sadistic behaviour with cats. Psychologists say that this stage of tormenting animals is transient but natural. Curiosity means that boys are more likely than girls to drop cats from heights to see if they land on their legs. (This was once taken to extreme when pilots – men of course – flying out of an airport on Long Island dropped cats from successive heights in competition to see who could drop a cat from the highest altitude with the cat surviving.)

It may be that boys inherit the vestiges of an instinctive desire to understand how animals behave, so that they will grow to be more efficient hunters. This is the reason that anthropologists use to explain why most cultures in the world keep animals as pets. While the pets are juvenile they are cared for and 'parented'. As adults they are often abused, tortured or simply allowed to die from neglect.

Western culture influences children's attitudes to cats. At least as far back as Aesop, animals have been used in children's literature to explain essentially human values. In one study of children's literature over half of all animal behaviour in stories was idealized and humanized. Realistic descriptions of cat behaviour occur even less frequently. No wonder some kids grow up thinking that cats talk, have jobs and always survive to feature in the next cartoon.

14. *I know I'm a child substitute. What happens after they have real human kids?*

Initially, cats often get demoted because the woman has so many more responsibilities. But then curious things happen. Cat owners swear that life won't change for them or their cats once children come along, but reality bites. There is no conceivable way that life does not radically change for people who have children. These changes apply to cats too.

People quite correctly try to avoid any abrupt changes in their cat's routine but, sooner or later, changes in routine and in attitude take place. The child substitute is now the potential child killer. This is a risky time for cats. Human parental instincts sometimes see other animals as greater threats than they really are. Mother fears that the cat will smother the baby, so the cat is denied access to the new baby's room. This should be done long before a baby comes home rather than as a direct result of the baby's presence. It is not uncommon for cats to be vanquished from the home, to sleep outdoors or to be rehomed.

After the initial, negative life changes of no longer being the centre of attention, a cat usually settles into a more aloof but equally comfortable existence as the children grow up. If it lives with a middle-class family it can expect to be played with more, comforted more and be a source of comfort more often than if it lives with a less well-advantaged family. It seems that in families lower down the social scale children don't know how to take advantage of a cat in their lives. This is more common with boys than girls. Girls, certainly those between nine and thirteen years old, according to one Canadian study, turn to their cats for emotional support, contact comfort, protection and reassurance much more readily than boys.

Cats become attachment figures for children and contribute to a child's basic sense of trust. According to Austrian studies, children who grow up with cats have more empathy with nature and with other animals – domestic or wild. Portuguese and American studies suggest that introducing a cat into the home of children with learning disabilities increases the child's attention span.

No matter how good cats are in this role they can never replace parents or other people as resources for caring and learning. In the distressing circumstances of sexual abuse, children find their cats very supportive while they navigate their way through their feelings of isolation and confusion. Autistic children also treat pet cats as extra special, displaying behaviour to them they don't display even to their families.

Many people feel that it is good for their children to be strongly attached to their cats, but this is not necessarily so. According to Dutch psychologists, eight-year-old children who are strongly attached to their cats have higher than average feelings of self esteem and self worth. Thirteen-year-old children who are strongly attached to their cats have lower than average self esteem and self worth. (A study of 1,300 households in the United States revealed that adults aged between thirty-five and forty-four who are strongly attached to their cats suffer more from depression than those less attached to their cats.)

15. *And once their children leave home, what happens to me?*

That depends overwhelmingly on the personality profile of the new 'empty nesters'. Some parents yearn so much for the freedom and independence they experienced before having children that they long for the cat to depart from this life, leaving them free to come and go as they please and to travel at will.

Many people go through this phase but women in particular find the absence of being needed very stressful. Rather than relaxing into parental 'retirement', life becomes meaningless. This happens to men too, but to a lesser degree. For example, on a stress scale of mid-life changes, women rank the loss of contact with their grown children far higher than men do.

After the initial sense of loss, some people turn to their cats for solace and comfort. The nest is empty but people have a lifelong need to nurture. Historically, parents continued to care for their young because their married children lived nearby. Grandparents were (and in many parts of the world still are) an integral part of the three-generation family. Historically they looked after the children while the parents hunted and gathered. With the dramatic changes in human lifestyles this century and the disintegration of the traditional family, the oldest generation no longer has the nurturing responsibilities it once had. In that sense cats are lucky because they are the beneficiaries of this change. After children leave home, a cat can become the centre of attention. But it runs the risk of being joined by more cats as its owners establish a new feline 'family'.

16. *Do people instinctively feel safer with me around, as they do with dogs?*

Apparently so. The dog's acute hearing and its willingness to alert the household when anything unexpected occurs are among the most common reasons for dog ownership. Over two-thirds of dog owners say they feel more secure when they are with their dogs. But over one-third of cat owners also say they feel more secure when with their cats, although they know their cats will not attack and defend as a dog – at least in fantasy – is capable of doing. There are other, more complex reasons why cats make people feel safer.

Contrary to popular belief, there are no major personality differences between cat lovers and dog lovers, or for that matter between pet owners and people who do not own pets, so there are no initial variations in people's attitudes.

Curiously, it is the cat's very muteness that is pivotal to making people feel comfortable, even protected. People use language to communicate but they also use it to deceive, misinform, criticize and insult. Cats seem just to listen. They don't judge, question or evaluate. How much they understand is irrelevant, since most cat owners feel their cats understand their emotions. This makes them feel more relaxed, content, safe and secure.

No other species of life on earth (except perhaps ants) keeps 'pets' – other animals that live commensally with them for their mutual benefit. Human pet keeping may be in part instinctive but it may also be a by-product of human consciousness – of human thought – a behaviour that softens some hidden internal conflicts associated with relationships. Cats, and dogs for that matter, are people's most cherished companions because they are so good at feeding people with non-verbal signs of affection. They make people feel respected, desired, needed, valued, wanted. The slightly detached contentment of a cat is enormously appealing to people though they don't know exactly why. Dogs make people feel safe and secure in obvious ways. Cats, being cats, do so in more mysterious but equally important ways.

CHAPTER TWO

The Secret Feelings and Emotions of Cat Owners

17. *Life is a delight. I am allowed to go where I want, when I want, and to do what I want. There is always food and warmth waiting for me back at home. But why must I wear a collar full of bells?*

People think that if a cat wears half a dozen bells on its collar birds will hear it coming. They forget that cats are cats, as graceful as any predator that ever moved. Any decent feline hunter soon learns how to silence even multiple bells.

The cat's utilitarian purpose is to kill. It does so superbly and efficiently. People first accepted cats into their permanent settlements perhaps 8,000 years ago, to act as rodent killers. Cats killed the mice and rats that thrived on stored grain and people appreciated their doing so. People hate mice and rats, but they like birds – even love birds. Today, very few people belong to organizations that protect rats and mice but many people belong to organizations that protect birds. Individual people and bird-loving organizations accuse cats of endangering birds, especially pretty birds or birds with beautiful songs. Beauty, be it through sight or sound, appeals to human senses – after all, this is why people are so attracted to cats. If cats, animals that prefer to march to their own tune, behaved as they do but had piggy little eyes and scaly tails people would certainly not keep them as favoured house pets. Forcing cats to wear bells is a curious human compromise. People feel that it allows a cat to behave as nature intended; to stalk small living creatures. At the same time, if the cat moves forward with any jerkiness of movement, the bird will hear danger approaching and fly away. In reality, bells are only occasionally useful but they salve many human consciences. For public relations purposes, if for no other reason, outdoor cats should continue to wear them.

18. *If I were as big as my African savanna relatives I'd look upon the people I live with as potential meals. So why do they call me Cuddles?*

Names can reveal the origins, aspirations, even the political leanings of people. Within each human culture people react very subjectively to different names. Among English names for humans, Adrian is considered artistic, Mary is thought to be quiet, Barbara is charming and Richard good looking. James and Elizabeth are dignified and aristocratic, while Kevin and Tracy are more relaxed and distinctly working class. Adding a 'y' or 'ie' to the end of a name changes its meaning. David is serious and sincere, Dave is strong and active while Davy is weak and passive.

Cats are often given descriptive names like Mischief, Dread, Slasher, Fang, Tigger, Blackie or Trouble. These names are based upon the appearance or behaviour of the cat, although they may also be aspirational if given to very young kittens. Cartoons, comic strips and films only marginally influence cats' names: Felix, Garfield and Sylvester – all cartoon characters – are uncommon cat names and are usually given to cats by children.

A cat's name often reveals the expectations of its owner. Some people acknowledge that a cat is a small but efficient predator and give names like Bandit. Affectionate names such as Cuddles, Treasure, Angel, Sunshine and Cupid carry the suggestion of parenthood and intimacy. These warm, loving names are very common, take many forms and are usually chosen by women. Some people actually find it easier or less embarrassing to use these affectionate names in public for their cats than they do for close friends.

19. *Why can't he admit he actually enjoys my company?*

Cats play several roles in people's lives. One of them is to act as an extension of the owner's personality. People like to project their own sexual image of themselves through the clothes they wear and cats are, to some extent, accessories to that image. This is why, historically, men in general prefer big, lean, muscular cats like panthers and pumas, lions and tigers while women, although attracted by the sensuousness of big cats, tend to prefer the more cuddly size of the domestic cat.

Middle-class man is different. He is usually university educated and is aware of his female as well as his male side. If he is confident in his sexual identity he is quite happy to be seen in public with a fluffy Persian, although deep in his heart he really only wants to be seen with a lanky Maine Coon. He may even take pride in the fact that he is seen in public with what is still, to many people, a feminine image. Of course, most men have no say in whether the family has a cat or even what type of cat it is. Most cats are acquired by the woman and children in the family. Given the opportunity, most men would select cheetahs and ocelots before Burmese and Domestic Short Hairs.

20. *I gaze out the window all day, my teeth chattering with frustration. Why won't they set me free?*

This is a relatively new phenomenon among cat owners and has its origins in the increasing emotional investment people are placing in their cats, and also in feelings of responsibility conscientious people have towards both their cat's physical wellbeing and the feelings of other people in the community. It is strictly a middle-class phenomenon.

There was a time, only a few years ago, when a cat was allowed to lead a cat's life. In the countryside, suburbia and small towns, virtually all cats lived in the garden and entered the house only for meals or for warmth. Each morning the cat wandered off to do its own thing which, in most instances, was to mark its territorial limits with urine and faeces, sleep in the warmth of the day and capture meals whenever possible. In between these activities it defended its territory or, if hormones demanded, sought a mate.

Unneutered males would get together in a benign 'brotherhood' and hang out in the territory of the queen in season, each calmly waiting his turn to mate with her. This 'brotherhood' never acted as a genuine pack, hunting and eating together; they simply acknowledged each other's existence. Life had few hang-ups. Cats had few behaviour problems because they were allowed to act like cats.

But society changed. In more and more families women as well as men went out to work. Changing lifestyles developed to the detriment of the more time-consuming dog but to the benefit of the more independent cat. Dog numbers declined while cat ownership literally exploded. Cats replaced dogs as the primary animal companions of many people. For the first time in history, large numbers of people became intimate with cats.

This increasing intimacy has brought with it a greater feeling of attachment and responsibility on the part of owners to protect their cats. That is why, increasingly, cats are jailed. People think that feeding their cat the best food and providing creature comforts – warmth, soft beds and fluffy toys – means that cats have landed feet first in heaven. They forget that these are but physical comforts. Increasingly, as people become more emotionally dependent upon their cats, even more felines will find themselves incarcerated in unnatural indoor homes, their teeth chattering in frustration as they observe living nature outdoors without being able to enter it.

21. *People are strange. One day I'm the most important thing in their lives. The next I'm kicked out of the house. Why are people so inconsistent?*

People have ambivalent feelings about cats. On one hand the pet cat is a true family member: it is fed, housed and cared for like other family members; it participates in family activities, from meals to watching television; sometimes it even accompanies families on holiday. People come to see their cats as individuals, different from all others – even from others of the same breed. People who live with cats eventually treat them as unique and irreplaceable individuals, worrying when their cats are unwell and mourning when they die.

On the other hand, cats are almost infinitely replaceable. In most countries there are always more cats looking for homes than there are homes available for cats. Cats have a set financial value and virtually anything with a finite value is replaceable. The legal definition of the cat clouds matters even more. In most cultures cats are classified as 'chattels', items owned by people. Until recently, in court cases, cat owners have been awarded only the replacement value of a cat after it has died or been lost through negligence. Recently, courts have modified their views and have also granted costs for 'loss of affection', but the general legal definition reinforces the concept that a cat is simply an item with a specific value.

The inconsistency in people's emotional attitude towards cats is still based on the prevailing feeling that the human is a distinct and unique species, separate from all others. This attitude is a relic from cultural history. Changes are gradually taking place and the feeling of domination and control over all animals, including cats, is being eroded and replaced by a feeling of responsibility towards other animals. In the near future, however, cats will continue to lead threatened lives; loved one day, abandoned the next.

22. *I live with a cataholic. Whenever she sees a stray cat she gets an impulsive desire to bring it home. Why?*

This can be simply the unalloyed care-giving response of natural nurturers, but it can also be the behaviour of people who find it difficult to communicate with other people and choose instead to surround themselves with animals. Although these people are reluctant to admit it, there is an element of power and control in their actions. They feel they cannot control their own or other people's lives, but in their chosen role of feline saviour all the rescued cats owe their lives and wellbeing to their rescuer.

Taken to an extreme, animal collecting becomes an addiction. Addictions to 'negatives' such as drug taking or gambling are widely acknowledged, but people can also develop addictions to healthy and rewarding activities such as sexual activity or care-giving. In the context of rescuing cats, these people fail to set limits to their behaviour and end up committing vast amounts of their time, energy and emotion to saving lost, abandoned or feral cats.

This can become obsessive and uncontrollable. A point is reached where animal collecting replaces relationships with other people. There simply is no time for human relationships and, if there is time, there is no emotional energy left. Eventually, stray cats replace intimate relations with people. Stray gatherers fulfil their need to be care-givers by investing all their time looking after lost cats. Because cats are almost always willing to accept a guaranteed and safe source of food and warmth, co-dependency develops. Carer and cat need each other and this leads to the repetitive, obsessive behaviour typical of all addicts. Cat addicts usually deny they are addicted to rescuing strays. They say they can control their habit, but they can't. In extreme cases, they stop taking care of their own personal hygiene and invest all their money and energy in caring for their cats. Breaking the habit is difficult, almost impossible, because of the powerful rewards and the constant supply of abandoned cats that 'need them'.

Animal addiction is far more common in women than in men and develops independently of class or financial worth. Cat rescue organizations are like honey pots to addicts. Detoxification and recovery is possible, but, as with all other potent addictions, difficult to complete. Relapses back into addiction are common.

23. *Every time she sees me I get dragged up to her mouth. Why does she always leave her lipstick on my head?*

A cat serves a variety of roles but for many people, and for women in particular, cats are there to be cared for, to be loved and nurtured. Even tough toms get kisses smack on the lips because they are human-baby sized. Women do this more than men because women are more nurturing. But that doesn't mean that men don't *want* to behave this way, it is just that in our culture some men are embarrassed to show their emotions.

Men may be uptight about showing emotions but, curiously, in public places like veterinary clinic reception rooms they are often more willing to show affection to their cats than they are to show affection to other humans. Men can be just as willing as women to stroke, cuddle and 'gentle' their cats. 'New Men' even kiss their cats in public.

People behave this way because, unlike virtually all other forms of life, they have a lifelong need to care for living things. This evolved from the need to care for their own infants over a protracted period of time, often amounting to decades. Kittens have fully developed brains by the time they are twelve weeks old. By twenty-four weeks they can take care of themselves and soon they become simply competition for their parents and siblings. Human brains take infinitely longer to develop. It takes eighteen years for some parts of the human brain to mature. In the survival of the fittest, nurturing was beneficial for both the parents and the young.

One of the problems people have, if you want to call it a problem, is that their need to nurture becomes universal. They care for their own families but they also care for other people, other animals and even plants. Kissing is just a visible sign of human caring but its origins show it had a practical purpose. In their evolutionary past – and in some cultures even today – mothers chewed up food and passed it to their babies with a 'kiss'. The human kiss has evolved into a symbolic gesture of attachment. Because cats bring back raw rather than regurgitated meat for their kittens, domestic cats fail to understand the significance of this human manifestation of affection.

24. *Will they be upset if I leave home?*

Yes, and innocence is a key factor. The domestic cat is a man-made creation, although it is true cats were originally self-domesticated. About 8,000 years ago, North African wild cats were attracted to sites of permanent human habitation because of the bountiful supply of mice and rats. In this new ecological habitat, survival of the fittest was responsible for the reduction in tooth and body size and for increased 'tameability'. For millennia cats bred according to these environmental pressures and to their own preferences, but more recently people have actively intervened in their choice of mates. This final stage of domestication, some people say, robbed the cat of the means by which it could take care of itself. This is why many people feel a personal responsibility for any stray or homeless cat.

There is a little theoretical mumbo jumbo in this hypothesis. Not all homeless cats are lost innocents. Wandering offers a vicarious thrill to most cats as it permits the individual to live by cat rules rather than human ones. The cat chooses its own latrine site, its own territory and its own friends. It is excited by the chance of finding its own food although it may prefer the chase to the meal itself.

Homeless people do not provoke a similar compassionate response because not all of them share the image of wide-eyed innocence that cats have. Those who are homeless through their own innocence are grouped together with those who are homeless through drug or alcohol abuse or, as is the case with some adolescents, for the excitement of living rough and snubbing the accepted precepts of their society. This latter group shares strong similarities with some stray young male cats but animal lovers fail to see this.

25. *Will people get upset when I die?*

Cats get upset when cats die and people do too. Cats are honest about their feelings. When cat-friends die, over half of all cats – fifty-two per cent – suffer from a decreased appetite. Fifty-one per cent vocalize more. Fifty-eight per cent demand more affectionate attention. Forty-one per cent seek out and rest in the deceased cat's favourite spot. These behaviour changes may last for as long as six months.

Most cat owners also get deeply upset when their cat dies although some, men in particular, try to hide their feelings. The death of a cat combines the loss of companionship, the interruption of routine and, in a curious way, the loss of innocence. All of these losses are very distressing.

People experience the same feelings of loss when their cats die as they do when close friends and relatives die. They may deny what has happened, get angry with themselves, their family or their veterinarian for allowing the death to occur, feel deep, inconsolable grief or the need to be alone, or demand constant emotional support. Life changes significantly. Some people find it difficult to concentrate – so difficult they cannot work. Eventually, with time, the loss becomes accepted and integrated into the cumulative experiences of life. In that sense the death has been a learning experience and the owner is able to reconstruct his or her life in the absence of the cat.

This process lasts for a varying length of time but on average it takes almost a year to complete. It is significantly different from the way people grieve when young friends and relatives die only in one aspect: when cats die there is little grieving for 'what might have been', one of the most potent aspects of the grief felt when children die.

Grieving may begin even before a cat dies, as soon as the veterinarian gives the 'bad news'. Once a person knows that their cat is fatally ill, that person's social life changes. It is not unusual for him or her to cancel engagements, work less efficiently, avoid holidays and concentrate all emotional energy on the cat. This is most likely to occur in people who have made a major emotional investment in their cat, perhaps because of a lack of contact, involvement and support from other people. In these circumstances, people are not only upset, they may be depressed, stop eating, find it difficult to speak to other people and find themselves incapable of coping with even minor responsibilities. This form of grieving is not unusual in compulsive care-givers. According to John Bowlby, the psychologist who first described the great importance of 'attachment', the compulsive care-giver satisfies his or her need for attachment by becoming a permanent 'giver' rather than a 'receiver'. He says, 'The person who develops in this way has found that the only bond of affection available is one in which he must always be the care-giver, and that the only care he can ever receive is the care he gives.' This is the personality type that suffers most when a companion cat dies.

Many cat owners, but especially those who buy books about the way their cats or they themselves behave, have made a significant emotional investment in their feline relationships. The loss, or even the anticipated loss of their cat, can create complicated, often prolonged reactions. This is a recognized phenomenon and organizations exist throughout North America, Europe, South Africa, Australia and Japan to offer support to grieving cat owners.

26. *Will my death have any effect on my human family?*

The death of a pet can be a milestone in the lives of many people. It is one occasion when barriers come down and true feelings are revealed. Symbolically, it can be a seminal event that ends one stage in the owner's life and initiates the next one.

Responding to an article on 'Handling the Death of a Pet' in the American magazine *Cat Fancy*, one reader described what happened when her cat died: 'We buried her in a special box with one of my husband Frank's old T-shirts that she loved. Just as I was covering her and closing the box, Frank appeared with one of her favorite toys. I have never been so touched by a simple gesture. I hadn't been crying but I started then. We cried together. Even in death, Jennie brought us a little closer.' As for many other cat owners, the writer's emotional relationships were profoundly affected not just by the death of her cat but by the circumstances that surrounded that emotional upheaval.

The emotional consequences when a cat dies depends upon the stage of life and specific circumstances of the individual person. My cat Blackie's death, when I was a child, was a 'rite of passage'. Her death, together with the death of my dog, Sparkie, were the first close deaths I experienced. Relatives had died but never before someone or something I lived with, played with, tickled, fed, comforted or sought comfort from. Symbolically, my cat's death was my loss of innocence, of childhood 'animal' innocence. In a peculiar way, the cat's death was a 'rite of passage' from the 'natural' life of childhood to the 'cultural' life of adulthood.

The death of a cat in the owner's late adolescence can be equally symbolic. The writer Gail Sheehy has described the 'passages' of life, the stages of emotional development that people go through. The average life expectancy of a cat is approximately the same as the length of these stages. People often remember the death of their cat as the time they left one stage and entered another: breaking the bonds of the family and embarking on an independent life; the maturing of children and their leaving home; the onset of feelings of mortality. A cat's death almost always has an emotional impact on a family although it is not always possible to prophesy what that impact will be.

27. *Why do people get embarrassed about their emotions when cats die?*

This is a unique aspect of the grieving process people experience when cats die. Over seventy-five per cent of cat owners are 'deeply distraught' when their cat dies, but most cultures have no accepted ways of coping with these feelings. The death of a close fellow human is an 'earth stopper' and, in response, each culture or society has developed rituals and customs to ease the pain. In virtually every civilization, a human death leads to open and genuine support from others. Immediately following a death both activity and communication increase. Emotional barriers are lowered and friends and relatives become less inhibited than usual. There is more physical contact, more touching and, of course, there is ceremony and ritual.

When a cat dies, the response is almost a complete reverse. Western religions – Judaism, Christianity and Islam – offer no rituals or ceremonies. (In contrast, Buddhism, Hinduism and more obscure but equally ancient Eastern religions such as Zoroastrianism, have time-honoured rituals that accompany animal death.) Activity decreases, if only because the cat-generated jobs of feeding and playing are no longer available. The emotional barriers around the family often remain, or are raised even higher when a cat dies. Visitors are less likely to call because they are embarrassed about how to behave. Instead of letters, flowers and phone calls, there is increased isolation and loneliness. Even within the family there may be less communication than normal. Routines are expected to continue as if nothing has happened.

Western cultures stipulate that the death of a cat should not even cause a hiccup in the flow of life. Yet those people who were close to the cat that died *know* how deeply they feel the loss, and it is this dichotomy that leads to embarrassment. 'How can I feel such emotional desolation over the death of my cat when I did not feel as bad when my relative died?' People ask themselves. Only recently have Western religions begun to acknowledge these feelings and create rituals for pet loss. The newest Western religion, Animal Rights, has the most advanced programme to help people cope with the death of their pets.

28. *I live in a three-dimensional world. So why do they always think I'm stuck when I'm up a tree?*

Other than mountain climbers, most people live in a two-dimensional world. So do their dogs for that matter. They think in two dimensions and find it difficult to understand that cats think in different ways. Height is important for cats; the cat that obtains the high ground is dominant in most meetings with other cats.

At one time in their evolution people were much better than they are now at climbing. Today they are overwhelmingly inferior to cats in this ability. Not only do cats have retractable claws to help them climb, they have a sense of balance that accommodates instantly subtle changes in their three-dimensional world. Because people find it difficult to comprehend that cats almost always find their way down after climbing trees, they panic and call for help. In these circumstances cats usually just climb higher. Cat skeletons are never found at the tops of trees unless they have been taken there by other predators.

29. *Will they always be annoyed if I bring death to their garden?*

Physical attractiveness is intensely important to people. That is why intelligent, affectionate and very trainable – but visually unattractive – rats are despised, while innocent-eyed, sensuous, blood-lusting cats may be loved, treasured and admired.

People like attractive people: a handsome man accused of murder is more likely to be found not guilty than an unattractive one; disruptive behaviour by an attractive child is more likely to be excused by the teacher than disruptive behaviour by an unattractive child; physically attractive politicians are more likely to win elections than less attractive ones.

The same human attitude applies to cats. Pure-bred cats, bred for coat colour, length and texture and for body shape and size, are almost universally bred for what people feel are 'good looks'. Physical attributes, like a multicoloured or dense coat to give camouflage or protect the cat from the elements, are now selectively enhanced to appeal to people's eyes and sense of touch.

Really good-looking cats can literally 'get away with murder' because of another human idiosyncrasy: curiously, people don't particularly like absolute perfection in other people, or in cats. They prefer perfection tinged with a little human weakness or, in the case of cats, reversion to feline instincts. In one lovely scientific study an American psychologist asked actors to answer an educational quiz and recorded their responses. Several actors were asked to answer questions equally correctly, but one of the actors was asked to make a noisy commotion then say, in an anguished tone, 'Oh my goodness, I've spilled coffee all over my suit.' That was the person who listeners to tapes of the conversations found most attractive.

A seductively pretty Chinchilla cat is admired for its physical perfection. But when it stalks and kills a bird, although its owner may be distressed, there is a deep-seated feeling of admiration that their pure-bred is not only pretty, but is still a cat. If a rat were to commit the same crime it would get far less consideration.

30. *What is more important to my owners, the length of my life or its quality?*

That depends upon the emotional investment a person has placed in a cat. Advances in medicine have made this a more relevant problem than it once was. Kidney failure, for example, a most common feline problem, can be treated in a variety of ways, all of which involve ethical and emotional decisions. Dialysis – flushing waste from the body – can be carried out in a number of ways but all of these are time consuming and, to use a medical term, 'invasive'. Even the most benign treatment, peritoneal dialysis, means that a cat's abdomen must be fitted with a permanent 'tap' to which the dialysis machine is attached for several hours each day. This will increase the quantity of life but what about the quality?

An alternative is to provide a kidney transplant. Technically, this is not a difficult surgical procedure but where does the kidney come from? Is it ethically acceptable to sacrifice one cat to obtain a kidney for another? The American veterinary schools which carry out feline kidney transplants attempt to calm their ethical conflicts by stipulating that owners of cats receiving kidney transplants must also provide a safe and secure home for the cat that has 'donated' the kidney.

Fortunately, the overwhelming majority of cat owners, even those with intense or dependent emotional relationships with their cats, do not find the quality or quantity problem difficult to answer. Almost invariably they make the decision for quality. If a cat with kidney failure will live longer on a low-meat diet but the cat is unhappy following such a regime, most owners will feed it what it wants – succulent rich meat – knowing that this shortens the cat's life but that it enjoys its remaining days.

One considerable area where quantity outweighs quality is the basic decision about whether to let a cat roam outdoors or restrict it forever to an indoor existence. Statistics are irrefutable: the cat's greatest predator is the motor vehicle. Over fifty per cent of urban outdoor cats will suffer a serious road-traffic accident at some time during their lives. Of these accidents, forty-two per cent are fatal. Each cat owner must calculate the risk to their cat according to where they live. Some will choose to allow their cat the freedom of movement that many cats want, knowing the risk of serious injury or death is high. Others find this risk too emotionally overwhelming and choose for length of life. This is a perfectly acceptable decision if it is made early in a cat's life and is augmented by the decision to devote time and energy to providing the house-bound feline with physical and psychological stimulation.

31. *Why am I not allowed in the nursery? All I want to do is have a good look and sniff.*

Some people fear that their cat is dangerous to their new child. One hideous fantasy has the cat cuddling up so closely to the new baby that it smothers it. Another has the cat, in a fit of jealous pique, attacking the baby. Both worries are unjustified although cats should never be left unattended with babies or young children.

The smothering scenario requires the cat to get into the baby's crib – something that any cat is liable, even likely, to do. While smothering is overwhelmingly unlikely, cats should be prevented from hopping into babies' cribs, either by restricting access to the nursery or by placing netting over the crib.

Jealousy is a feline behaviour but it is unlikely to be directed at a baby. Cat owners should try as best they can to continue with old feline routines when a new baby enters a household. They should anticipate unavoidable changes and alter routines before the actual arrival of the baby. For example, the nursery should become 'off limits' months before the new baby appears.

Cats are unlikely to bite or scratch babies in their cribs. It is only when infants are moved to the floor, to the cat's own territory, and begin to crawl, that they are at risk from cats. Curiously, people who have been virtually paranoid about the danger to their baby in the crib fail to see the increased danger as their infant becomes active and mobile.

32. *When I was first introduced to my home, the adults told the children that I had been bought for them. Is it really true that I'm simply an amusement for a bunch of kids?*

Yes and no. Cats are, in part, toys – though different from dolls and teddy bears in that they bleed and die. Children graduate from satin-edged blankets, to stuffed toys, to cats. The unfortunate aspect of this development is that, although all of these items are deeply important to children, parents sometimes think of each one as being equally expendable. Parents get cats for their children's amusement. After all, if the child is playing with the cat the parent has more time to get on with other jobs. It is very likely, however, that although they do not consciously acknowledge the fact, parents are saying something important to their children when they bring a cat into the home. In this sense cats are not simply childhood amusements.

Sensible parents tell their children that they are responsible for their cat. Unless a child is emotionally very mature, this is simply not true. Parents are responsible for the physical and emotional wellbeing of family cats. Yet, this standard parental proclamation is often the first intimation children have of their responsibility towards living things. When a parent introduces a cat into the home, saying 'its for the children', what he or she is really saying is 'I think being a parent is important and I want my child to start learning that now.'

In all cultures, from wealthy and sophisticated to more primitive and basic, women and children are responsible for pets. In hunter/gatherer societies, children learn about animal behaviour at least in part through pets. In our society they have an early opportunity to learn about their later responsibilities to the living world around them.

33. *I'm a cat. I have feelings and emotions. I feel frustrated if I'm left jailed at home. Why should I be treated like a stuffed toy or a learning experience?*

Because, until very recently, most people denied that cats were aware of their own feelings and emotions. Many still find it difficult to accept that cats have emotions. They like to think that every response a cat makes is instinctive; a reflex wired by evolution into its brain. They like to think that cats work on autopilot, without too much thinking or feeling. Veterinarians know that cats have feelings and emotions, in part because they have had the opportunity to observe so many, but also because they know that drugs used to treat psychosomatic disorders in people – problems like clinical anxiety or compulsive behaviour – work in cats too.

By denying cats, or any other animals for that matter, the 'human' ability of consciousness, people separate themselves from the rest of the living world. And, once separated, the rest of the world can be treated differently. Cats become expendable items of light relief, with purely financial, rather than intrinsic, value. The greater the financial value the less expendable the cat becomes, which is why pure-breds are less likely to be allowed into the dangerous outdoors than random-bred cats.

34. *Why does she take me to the vet every time I wink? Is she compulsive?*

Definitely a worrier. Possibly an exaggerated motherer. Maybe she is not getting enough emotional nourishment anywhere else and is reciprocating in the only way she knows how. Other emotionally malnourished people become obsessive feeders, bloating their cats with calories of love.

Some people, perfectly sensible when it comes to the health of their children, overreact when their cat is apparently unwell. If a child is itchy or has diarrhoea or has vomited, parents take simple remedial action. But if the cat is itchy, has the runs or vomits, it means an instant trip to the vet. One simple explanation is that people are better at understanding human medical complaints than they are at understanding what to do when their cat has the blues. They forget that the principles of care are exactly the same: prevent the problem from getting any worse; eliminate the cause; promote recovery and repair.

Natural born worriers will obtain professional advice just as quickly for their cats as their children. Obsessive and compulsive medical seekers are the same; so too are ardent mother-ers. The emotionally malnourished are different. These people use the cat as a ticket of admission to talk to the veterinarian, someone they see as compassionate and understanding; a good listener. The cat's problem may be trivial – licking its bottom or nails needing a trim – but it provides a valid reason for an appointment. There is a degree of learned helplessness in this behaviour. The cat owner visits the vet and gets a personal emotional reward because the vet listens and appears to care. Now that the owner knows that this is available she is even more willing to call the vet the next time her cat has the slight-est change from normal. The behaviour is self rewarding and, in that sense, becomes compulsive.

CHAPTER THREE

The Secret Foibles of Cat Owners

35. *Until recently I enjoyed digging in the carpets and climbing the curtains. I can't any more and the reason why is horrific. They say they love me but, before I knew what was happening, my family had all my front toes amputated. Why did they do that to me?*

People have their cats declawed for thoughtless and totally self-ish reasons. Caring cat people would never amputate a cat's toes if they paused and pondered over exactly what they were doing. Curiously, declawing cats is a cultural phenomenon: it is a normal procedure in some countries and a heinous activity in others.

People best understand this operation when they look at their own hands and nails. Removing the claws is not the same as just pulling human nails out. If that were all that was done the nails would simply grow back. Declawing involves removing the nail and the bone the nail grows from. Concerned vets tried to develop an alternative procedure – just cutting the muscles that extend the claws – but this turned out to have drawbacks. Others invented artificial blunt-tipped nail-covers to glue periodically over the nails.

A cat's claws are not simply weapons, they are nature's original Velcro. Each pin-point sharp claw has individual muscles to extend or retract it, allowing cats to live in a three-dimensional world, climbing trees or gluing themselves in their cat baskets when they visit vets. If a cat slips while walking on something high up, it uses its claws to scramble back to where it was. Of course, if a cat enters a demarcation dispute with another cat, its claws are superb at holding on to its opponent but its teeth do most of the damage.

Cats also use these sophisticated utensils for marking a territory, leaving scratch marks on visible objects to signal their presence to other cats. It doesn't matter whether there are other cats around or not, all cats potentially behave this way. That is why cats like to scratch the arms of sofas, legs of tables or carpet at the top of the stairs. All of these are in highly visible places.

By starting early, and by providing a cat with scratching material that it finds attractive, most household damage can be controlled. People often forget that a scratching post must be placed in a very visible location, initially in the centre of the room. People who keep cats indoors need to use what animal trainers call aversion therapy: if a cat scratches where it should not scratch it is squirted with a water pistol or zapped with a rape alarm. When it scratches on its approved post it gets rewarded.

36. *People in North America and northern Europe have similar attitudes towards animal welfare. So why are amputations strictly a North American phenomenon?*

It is a cultural thing – if you include finance in culture. In Ontario, one of the world's heartlands of bunny-hugging animal-rights awareness, over 100,000 cats have their front toes amputated annually. In France, Germany, Spain or Britain the operation is seldom, if ever, carried out.

There are two bottom lines to this human dilemma. The first is furniture damage. Cat owners give many reasons for wanting the amputation to be carried out, but almost invariably they are anxious to protect their furniture from cat scratching. Although the operation is a rather draconian mutilation, it does have strong hidden rewards for the amputees; seventy per cent of Ontario cat owners report a closer attachment to their cats after declawing. In addition, respected cat behaviourists report neither increases nor decreases in behaviour problems, including biting, after declawing.

The other bottom line is the veterinarian's vested interest. Again, in Ontario, veterinarians estimate that forty per cent of owners of declawed cats would no longer own their cats if they had not been declawed. One paper in a respected veterinary journal estimated that 40,000 cats would lose their homes yearly if they were not declawed.

When asked, four per cent of owners actually claimed they would not have kept their cats had they not been declawed. Ontario veterinarians, simply observers of the relationship between owner and cat, see the problem as ten times more important than Ontario cat owners. Perhaps this is because declawing is such a significant component of practice procedures and income. In other regions, where declawing has never been a significant part of veterinary work, vets are much less concerned that cats will be abandoned if they are not declawed. And in these regions, the real level of cat abandonment because of household damage is probably closer to the owners' four per cent than the veterinarians' higher estimate.

37. *Hollywood loves dogs: Lassie, Rin Tin Tin, Benji, Beethoven. Hollywood is a dog's best buddy. But cats? Nothing. At best we're the companions of baddies. Why does Hollywood treat me and my brethren so poorly?*

You hit the nail on the head when you described Hollywood as the dog's *best buddy*. In Hollywood's eyes cats cannot be buddies. Put another way, cats are not masculine, cats are feminine. And that's a negative.

Think about how Hollywood portrays dogs. In vintage movies, from *Rin Tin Tin* through the Lassie films to *The Incredible Journey*, dogs are stoic, solid, reliable and dependable. They fight for law and order. They save lives. In modern films, dogs actually become true best buddies. In *Turner and Hooch* and *K9*, dogs are unwavering, permanent, honest friends. And all they want for their services is a slap on the back and a 'Well done!'. Dogs are men.

Now consider the cat's role in Hollywood: the evil Donald Pleasence's accomplice in the James Bond film *You Only Live Twice*; the even more dastardly Charles Gray's accomplice in *Diamonds Are Forever*; Gayle Hunnicutt's horror cats in *Eye of the Cat*; the petulant troublemaker in *Babe*. According to Hollywood, cats are slinky, sensuous, spiteful, deceitful and manipulative. Cats are women.

It is not Hollywood that has created these stereotypes; male and female stereotypes already exist in all cultures. And it is not that Hollywood has created images for dogs and cats. It has merely taken accepted images and perpetuated them. From time to time Hollywood breaks away from stereotype, as in *Harry and Tonto*, a gentle film about an elderly man, evicted from his New York home, who travels to Chicago accompanied by his ginger tabby. But this is an exception, not the norm. Hollywood will continue to portray cats as accomplices of deceit until the market it caters for changes its attitude to cats.

38. *Why doesn't she know that I know her threats are empty ones?*

People make a common and simple mistake with cats; they think of them in human terms. As with humans, people give conditional warnings, but these are not understood by cats and owners usually fail to carry out the threatened discipline: 'If you climb that curtain once more you are banished from this house FOREVER.' Nothing happens. Upon finding the arm of the new sofa converted to a mass of shredded Draylon, the cat owner takes its cat to the scene of the crime and admonishes, 'If you do this once more, I'll have your guts for garters!' All the cat knows is that its owner is being unfriendly.

Cats understand that threats are empty because they are neither appropriate nor given at the right time. Cats respond best to something unpleasant happening WHILE it is doing what it is doing. For example, if an owner sees their cat climbing the curtains, the person squirts the cat with a water pistol. If it digs in house plants, set mousetraps under newspaper and place the potted plant on top. When the cat steps on the paper, pressure sets off the traps and throws the paper up around it. If it claws furniture, people should keep coins in an empty aluminium can and shake it or even throw it near the cat. If it climbs on the kitchen work surface, leave pots and pans so precariously placed that they clatter to the floor. Better yet, apply double-sided sticky tape for the cat to land on. It will hate the sticky feeling. If the cat jumps on beds, leave a cheap but effective pressure sensor alarm on the bed that sets off a screech for thirty seconds. People should be inventive with their discipline. Threats only diminish the relationship between people and their cats, aversion therapy actually diminishes the unacceptable behaviour.

39. *Do people really think I have supernatural abilities?*

In the seventeenth century, Europe and New England became enthralled by witchcraft. Witches were accompanied by a 'familiar' – a supernatural servant – which often took the form of a cat. Although the idea of witches and witchcraft remains today only in the minds of a small minority of people, a much larger number of people still associate cats with the supernatural.

The most common manifestation of this idea is the concept that cats have nine lives. People use this cultural 'artefact' to explain how cats survive what would otherwise be lethal accidents – falling from windows, dog bites, air-rifle wounds and road-traffic accidents.

A cat's survival is really predicted by its anatomy and physiology. A fall that would kill a heavier dog or human may only stun a lighter and more supple cat, or perhaps dislocate a joint. Lack of food and water leads to rapid dehydration, kidney failure and death in people. Cats can survive without sustenance for three or four times as long as people can before their kidneys fail irreversibly. People, and dogs for that matter, readily feel pain and show it through their actions and sounds. Cats may feel pain just as deeply but their own painkilling system, their endorphins, is superb and responds instantly. A painful injury that causes circulation failure and shock in people (and dogs) does not necessarily induce clinical shock in cats. Cats are built to survive injuries that might kill other animals.

Just as important to the concept of 'nine lives' is the fact that cats do not necessarily learn from their experiences. A cat might survive a long fall from an open window, but the next time it sees a sparrow land on the ledge it might make the same mistake again, and survive again. Its survival is not supernatural – it is the result of superb engineering.

40. *Why do some people hate cats but love dogs? After all, both of us are simply successful carnivores who enjoy the company of humans.*

This human foible is partly intuitive and partly cultural. In human evolution, people lived without domesticated animals for the first 99.7 per cent of their existence. Between 10,000 and 15,000 years ago, the greatest cultural change that ever affected humans occurred. Men willingly reduced the time they spent hunting and killing individual animals and increased their time spent caring for groups of animals and killing them selectively. Wolf-dogs had already moved into human settlements and were there to assist herd management. After all, the wolfs social behaviour had programmed it for domestication, to work with people. Dogs were, and still are, useful. They might want to share in the meat but they willingly eat bits that people don't want and act as resident sanitary engineers, tidying the human settlement.

Cats never shared this close relationship with people. Although the Egyptians trained cheetahs to assist in the hunt, generally speaking cats were unwanted visitors in human settlements. Big cats were downright dangerous. Smaller cats killed small domestic animals like newborn piglets or lambs. People put up with cats only because they reduced vermin in granaries. Until very recently cats remained solitary hunters, aloof, independent carnivores quite unlike willingly submissive dogs. Intuitively, people were drawn to the dog's social behaviour but not to the cat's apparent selfishness. Even today more people instinctively understand dogs better than cats. Many find cats quite mysterious. Mystery can be attractive but it is appealing to fewer people than understanding.

Attraction to dogs and antipathy to cats is also cultural. This dichotomy is most obvious in the differences between Christian and Islamic attitudes to dogs and cats: in Christian countries dogs are more likely to be revered and cats hated; in Islamic countries the reverse is true. This is because early Christians associated cats with devil worship and in Europe the cat has suffered unfairly ever since. Early in the history of Islam, Moslems conquered Persia, obliterating the dominant dog-loving Zoroastrian religion and driving survivors into India. Just as the ancient Hebrews made idolatry, the religion of the Egyptians, the most potent of sins, so too the early Moslems turned the dog, an image of Zoroastrianism, into a cultural taboo. With the dog relegated to the cultural sidelines, the cat moved up several notches on the ladder of respect in Islamic countries, but even so a number of people in these countries still have an innate feeling of unease in the presence of cats.

41. *If people are trying to take the wildness out of me and make me a cuddly, safe companion why are they trying to breed me with wild cats?*

This is a strange human desire. People intentionally breed cats for companionship. As the cat increasingly becomes the pet of the future, even more people will want individuals that are companionable, sociable, reliable, dependable and dependent. People want cats that they can control, not cats that march to their own tunes.

Human nature is such that not all people have the same aspirations for their cats. Some people thrill to the thought of living with a genuinely 'wild' animal. They see themselves as privileged observers of nature, of which their cat is but one natural part. Some of these people feel that centuries of select-ive breeding, while increasing the cat's willingness to live within human habitations, has diminished its natural looks. They feel that by breeding domesticated cats with 'wild' cats like the Afri-can Jungle Cat, *Felis chaus*, or the Indian Leopard Cat, *Felis bengalensis*, it will be possible to reintroduce anatomical and coat varieties that have been 'lost' through domestication.

There are many wild cats the same size as the domestic cat. None of them, other than perhaps the African Jungle Cat, has in its behavioural repertoire, a profound inclination towards domestic life. None of these cross breedings has, as yet, pro-duced a line as reliable as already exists, although these matings have produced distinctive coat colours and varieties.

42. *Is there any breed I should be to appeal to a man?*

An interesting answer comes from advertisements in men's fashion magazines such as *Esquire* and *GQ*. The only breed ever advertised in magazines such as these is the lanky, luxurious Maine Coon. That does not mean that this is the only breed that appeals to men.

A first question to answer is what type of man does a cat want to live with? Heterosexual men like their cats to be big, even thuggish. Cats with 'wild' looks are most appealing. This often means dense coats, like the Maine Coon's, but also the Norwegian Forest Cat, Siberian Forest Cat and even the Somali. Traditional heterosexual men, certainly those with tattoos on their shell-suited arms, don't much like Persians.

Homosexual men admire all these cats but are also attracted to the wide variety of other shapes and sizes. Dependent cats are almost universally admired because they are willing to receive the emotional investment that homosexual men invest in them. Caring for a cat is one way that a gay couple can reinforce their commitment to each other. They 'parent' their cat in a deeply caring way, attending to its personal hygiene, diet and medical care. When you get right down to basics, men are just about as good cat carers as women. If a cat wants to appeal to as many men as possible it should be stocky, cocky and enjoy a little arm wrestling.

43. *If I'm so good for people and they love me so much, why am I left alone when they go on holiday?*

Some people have ambivalent feelings towards cats. They do not feel as responsible for cats as they do for dogs and regard cats as being 'only part domesticated'. By that they mean that a cat is content to live with a human family but when that family leaves, the cat is capable of living on its own. Unfortunately, this is mostly true.

The domestic cat is still very close to its wild roots in Africa. Statistics suggest that well over half of all domestic cats throughout the word are 'feral', that they have reverted to living on their own wits, finding their own food and shelter, dependent upon no one. Unless selective breeding dramatically alters a cat, as it does for example in creating the Peke-faced Persian, any cat is theoretically capable of looking after itself.

That does not mean that without early learning and practice a cat is really capable of capturing or otherwise finding its own meals. People should not leave cats to fend for themselves when they go on holiday, but there is little wrong with leaving a cat at home alone as long as arrangements are made for a friend to visit each day, provide fresh food and water and play with the cat if it wants to play. (Dogs should never be left in these conditions but then dogs are pack animals that crave contact with other living beings, especially other dogs or people.) Most cats are quite capable of creating their own entertainment, independent of their owner's presence.

44. *I am descended from an elegant line of lone hunters. My meals are too small to share with others. Why do they think I want a cat companion?*

People live in social groups and feel that their pets should live with their own kind as well. This is absolutely true for dogs but not necessarily so for cats.

The cat is a solitary hunter and it is also correct that the meals it captures are fit only for one stomach. It is a loner by nature, sociable only through recent environmental pressures and selective breeding. Cat sociability increases when there is a large source of food nearby. In these circumstances large numbers of cats will live within easy access of that food. The colony will consist of related females, mothers and daughters, together with aunts and female cousins. The related males usually live around the periphery of the colony. New members are admitted because they are born into the family. As the males reach sexual maturity, they are usually driven away to join the male 'brotherhood' that surrounds the colony. These are the natural circumstances under which cats willingly live together.

Under the artificial circumstances of feline house arrest, a cat looks upon its home and garden as its own territory. In most instances, the sudden arrival of another cat on that territory, no matter how young the new cat may be, is seen as a territorial transgression. The resident does not see the newcomer as a potential friend. It is an unwanted interloper.

In some circumstances, the arrival of a new cat is just cause for the resident to pack its bags and leave, especially if it knows of another cat-free home within its extended territory. People can reduce the shock of the new by carefully considering whether it is in their cat's interest for a new cat to enter the home. When new cats do so (and under the right circumstances a good number of resident cats learn that a newcomer is not as bad as it first appeared), owners should firmly control all meetings. The resident should be permitted to inspect the sleeping newcomer, not the other way around. They should be kept in separate rooms for a period of days, sometimes even weeks, only coming near each other when they are fed on either sides of a closed door.

By gradually exposing the resident to the presence of the newcomer under benign circumstances, it is often possible to break down a cat's natural reluctance to share its home with another cat. Cats are not as concerned when new people enter their homes because, although people are moderately good cat substitutes, cats know they are really no competition at all.

45. *People seem so ungrateful. Why don't they appreciate the gifts I bring them?*

This is really odd. On one hand, people complain that cats are selfish, egotistical and self-centred. Yet at 6 a.m. after a successful hunt, when a cat triumphantly drops a half-dead mouse on its owner's pillow, its owner is upset. This is because people do not always understand or appreciate cat logic.

Early morning gifts vary according to the abilities or lifestyle of individual cats. Frogs, toads, salamanders, mice, small rats, grasshoppers, butterflies and multitudes of birds are presented to sleeping owners at dawn every day. This is actually odd because, in its relationship with its owners, the cat is the 'kitten' and the owners are the 'mothers'. In feline terms it is the 'mother' that brings food back for the 'kitten', not the reverse.

There is no easy answer to the hunter's behaviour. Only the gift giver really understands why it is bringing home such delectable gifts to share with its human family. People who find this natural behaviour unpleasant should simply avoid the possibility by keeping their bedroom door shut and the windows closed or screened. Under these circumstances, a cat will store its cadavers, often in neat rows, in a part of the garden it chooses as its larder.

46. *They got me when they first married. Now they don't want me. Why, and what can I do?*

Marriage creates a small social unit, a pack, as it were. Participants are no longer alone. Marriage provides relatively reliable access to physical contact, talk and sex, all of which are potent human needs. It increases the likelihood that both aspects of 'attachment' – care-giving and care-receiving – will be met.

Nurturing is a lifelong human behaviour. At the time of marriage, both for hormonal and social reasons, human couples feel this need most intensely. Cats can parasitize these human feelings because, as Konrad Lorenz so eloquently explained over fifty years ago, when people see a living creature with babyish features they feel an automatic surge of disarming tenderness. This is the young married couple's reaction to a kitten.

Today, young couples marry but often postpone having children. However, their need to nurture remains intense and physical and behavioural features of kittens and cats trigger a release for this feeling. All humans, but especially those who are primed and waiting to produce their own young, feel affection for animals with large eyes, bulging craniums and retreating chins. Humans respond in a caring, parental way to animals with bulging cheeks, elastic limbs and clumsy movements. That is why virtually all human cultures willingly care for young infant animals but only a few cultures translate this apparent affection to all adult animals.

Married couples acquire cats to 'complete' the family unit. Having a living thing to care for together reinforces their bonds with each other. But eventually they produce the real product, their own child. Some of these people then see the cat for what it really is; a rather poor substitute for the most potent care-releaser. Parents instinctively protect their own children, their own genes. Quite suddenly, for some of these parents, the lovable kitty becomes a potential sabre-toothed tiger, a risk to their progeny.

Fortunately, this emotional swing in attitude, although not uncommon, is usually temporary. People simply need to relax and see their situation in perspective. Given a little time they usually realize it is possible to transfer their nurturing to their child while still sharing part of it with their original child substitute.

47. *I'm independent, not a slave. Why do they put me in a harness and walk me like a dog?*

This is a characteristic of people whose feelings of attachment to their cat remain intense and who want to ensure that their cat has exposure to nature, but under safe and controlled circumstances.

In North America and Europe there are many 'new' cat owners whose previous experience with pets has been restricted to dogs. Their experience tells them that animals on leashes are safe and secure while freedom of movement brings risk and potential anguish. For various reasons, most of which are related to social trends, these people would like to have dogs but cannot, so they get cats instead. Many have heard that 'foreign' breeds like the Siamese are the most dog-like, and acquire them. They have also heard that these cats are happy to walk on leashes. This is not necessarily so.

Although some cat breed clubs profess that their breed is happy to walk on a leash, there is no evidence to suggest that love of leash walking is genetic. It is almost wholly a learned behaviour. Cats will walk on leashes if as kittens, preferably as early as six or seven weeks old, they are introduced to gardens and parks while on harnesses and leashes.

48. *Why have I been injected with a microchip? Nobody is ever going to know it's there.*

This is not as silly an idea as it appears to be. The facts are plain: some cats get lost; some do not actually get lost but rather, of their own free will, move house and take up residence with neighbours; some cats actually get stolen. And, unfortunately, a large number of cats are killed in road traffic accidents and their bodies are retrieved by local sanitation departments.

Many cats look remarkably similar to each other and if a cat loses its collar and name tag its chance of being positively identified is left to luck. In response to the problem of reliable identification, manufacturers invented a small, inert glass capsule, the size of a rice grain, that includes an information-carrying transponder. This 'rice grain' of information is injected just under the skin of a cat's neck where it rests permanently, without migrating elsewhere. Because the transponder is glass and inert the cat's body does not react to it. It does not bother the cat and the information in the transponder is 'read' simply by passing a 'reader' over the cat's body. If a transponder resides under the cat's skin the 'reader' finds it and prints out the information.

Microchips are cheap, easy to install, non-irritating and permanent. The information is almost impossible to tamper with. Government departments and ministries of agriculture are so impressed that from Japan, through Europe, to North America, systems are being developed to inject microchips into all livestock and use the transponders to track animal movements from farm to farm and eventually to abbatoirs.

In many countries the major dog shelters scan all incoming dogs for microchips and the system works quite well. Cat shelters have been slower to invest in this method of identification but the values for cats are perhaps even greater than for dogs.

Microchips can be used to identify lost cats but are useful in other ways too. It is not unknown for two families to dispute the ownership of a peripatetic cat. Both sincerely believe that they 'own' the cat and true identity can be proved through microchip identification. Many owners face the emotional trauma of never knowing what has happened to their straying cat. Microchips allow municipal roads departments to identify accurately the remains of road traffic accidents. And, because it is such an accurate method of identification, it would be thrilling to hear the story of a cat that travelled hundreds of miles across rivers, mountains and roads to be reunited after accidental separation from its family, where the cat was accurately identified by its microchip implant.

49. *I look around at other cats and all I see is fat, fat, fat. Why are so many of my feline friends getting fatter?*

It's not just because cat food tastes so much better than it once did. And it's not just because cats are becoming increasing sedentary because of decisions that people, not cats, make. The number of fat cats will continue to rise because of human demographics and emotions.

Veterinarians estimate that at least one third of all cats are clinically overweight. Pet-food manufacturers realize that this makes for an excellent market and have responded to the epidemic of feline obesity by producing a vast range of low-calorie tinned and dry foods. Usually called 'light', these foods increase their market share each year.

Fat cats are wholly a human creation and their perpetuation lies in the hidden role cats play in many people's lives. Cats are smaller than people but have more willpower. They set battle plans and carry them through.

For a housebound cat, denied the physical and emotional thrills of stalking prey, eating food becomes one of life's greatest pleasures. Food becomes an obsession. The cat knows that people control the supply of food; the cat knows how to control people. It chooses moments of human weakness, such as at dawn when the human mind is a blur. The foody cat jumps on its owner while the owner is in bed and walks on her face. It vocalizes in a plaintive but sufficiently strident manner to prevent sleep. If it is inventive it dips its paw in its water bowl, hops back to the bed and shakes its wet paw in its owner's face. The cat gets fed.

Foody cats monitor all individuals in the household and determine who are the weak links, the easiest marks. These are usually men. When this person appears, the cat sensuously rubs its body against the weak link's leg, purrs seductively, stares deeply and unblinkingly into the weak link's eyes – and gets fed.

The weak link gives the cat extra food because he finds it difficult to show his emotions, to be physical, to touch. He doesn't do these things with his family. With his children, he expresses his affection by giving them money, but with his cat he offers sardines and chicken. That is why the level of obesity in the cat population remains large but in the future it will increase for other reasons.

In many countries, including the United States, Canada and Britain, cats have superseded dogs in actual numbers. The cat is the pet of the future. Many of these new cat owners have acquired purebred cats, often at considerable expense. These cats are likely to be restricted to life indoors, which is boring, so food becomes more appealing. But, just as significantly, most of these cats will be neutered. Increasingly, most cats – whether they live indoors or outdoors – will be neutered and neutered cats, in general, weigh more than unneutered ones. This is the most significant reason why cats will go to fat in the future.

50. *Why does she think I love her more than her husband does?*

People feel that a cat's love is unconditional, pure and everlasting. The life-long 'kitten' in cats, the purring and rolling, the pleasure sounds, the joyous body language, all of these create a feeling of unquestioning devotion, an absence of judging, total trust, unspoken understanding – of boundless adoration and love. The pet cat's apparent love and contentment is 'superabundant', greater than is possible in any adult human relationship, and fills a subconscious void in people's lives. A husband can love just as deeply but is no competition for this fantasy.

51. *Why have they left me with the kids. Isn't that irresponsible?*

Yes, it is irresponsible. This is an education phenomenon. The more advanced the education of the parents the less likely it is that a cat will be left with the children.

People say they get cats for the children. Many understand that while caring for a cat is an excellent learning experience, it remains the parent's responsibility to care for the feline. This is a healthy attitude. It means that parents understand that a cat is not simply a toy; it is not an item to be discarded. Sensible parents never leave children unattended with cats. They never agree to look after a neighbour's cat then give the cat to the children to care for. They understand that cats have their own individual needs but also that cats need monitoring and that only adults should be in charge of them.

This behaviour pattern requires some thought on the part of people and is more likely to occur amongst those with either a university education or an inherent desire to learn and to understand, a desire that has led to that person reading and learning in the absence of the availability of higher education. Irresponsibility will always be a facet of the behaviour of certain people. These individuals remain irresponsible regardless of education. For many others, the road to increased responsibility for cats remains in people understanding the cat's specific needs.

52. *If so many people love cats so much why do so many of my relatives have to fend for themselves?*

Let's start with a little terminology. Wild cats are cats that were never domesticated, either self-domesticated or through active human intervention. In Europe, the European Wild Cat, which lives in remote areas such as the Scottish Highlands and Eastern Europe's Carpathian Mountains, is seldom seen by people and never kept as a pet. In Africa and parts of Asia, the African Wild Cat continues to live on its own. Thousands of years ago it was the founding stock for the domestic cat.

The domestic cat lives with people. Some domestic cats have fallen fully under human control and are recognized as distinct breeds. The majority, however, continue to find their own mates and to breed selectively according to their own needs. These are the world's house cats, individuals that live with people and, to a considerable extent, rely upon people for their welfare.

Finally, there are feral cats. These are descendants of domestic cats that either of their own free will or through accidents of fate have found themselves fending for themselves as their wild cat ancestors once did. On remote subantarctic islands feral cats survive by eating birds. In the Galapagos archipelago they eat freshly hatched turtles as they crawl towards the sea. Near Japanese fish-processing plants they live in massive numbers eating fish waste. In central London or Paris or Philadelphia they survive on mice, rats and McDonalds.

Cat lovers feel that these feral cats lead strenuous and difficult lives. Because they are only familiar with their dependent domesticated relatives they think that feral cats are helpless without human intervention. This is not true.

Of all mammals, cats are among the most fascinating to

observe from an evolutionary perspective. First of all, they have been brilliantly adaptive in hitching themselves to humans, the dominant species on the planet. This helped them migrate to and settle in all parts of the world. Cats are also, genetically speaking, magnificently adaptive. When cats got into cold storage meat warehouses in Chicago at the turn of the century, eighty per cent of the cats soon died. But those that survived mated and within two generations the cold storage cats were much smaller and had denser coats than their forebears. They adapted to their environment. So too did the cats that eat birds on distant Marrion Island or the cats that eat McDonalds in Memphis.

There is nothing wrong with cats fending for themselves. In fact, there are potent arguments that they should be encouraged to do so. As cats adapt to their new environments they naturally select the best genes for survival in their new homes. This is natural selection at its best, rather than the human imposed selection for coat colour or intensity of voice. People can love their own cats while at the same time admiring, but not overwhelmingly interfering with, their pet cat's feral relatives.

53. *What bothers them so much when I mark my territory with urine, faeces and scratching posts?*

People like their pets to be attractive, appealing and innocent. Quite simply, they do not like their pets to be destructive. Except for some adolescent human males, people do not mark their territories with their urine. Except on the fringes of Western cultures, people do not leave their faeces in public places. Except for society's disrespected vandals, people do not despoil their buildings and monuments. In some people's eyes cats that spray urine, defecate in the front garden and scratch the furniture are anti-social because in human terms these are overwhelming marks of disrespect. They fail to understand that in feline terms this behaviour is a sign of social communication, as important to cats as shaking hands and idle chat are to people.

54. *Why do some humaniacs think that I want to be 'free'?*

Within the animal loving human population there are degrees of respect for animals. Most people agree that animal 'welfare' is a human responsibility. Increasingly, large numbers of individuals feel that animals have basic 'rights'; for example, freedom from pain, torture and neglect. Some people also feel that all animals, including domestic dogs and cats, should be 'liberated' from the slavery of ownership.

Animal liberationists believe that any form of ownership is a form of slavery. A domestic cat that lives with people, the liberationist argues, is living an unnatural existence. All cats, they say, should be given the opportunity to return to nature, to breed at will and to live independently of human intervention.

This Thoreau-like dream is mesmeric to some. But in their desire to recreate Utopia they forget that there never was such a place. Evolution is not static. It is constant and is going on before people's eyes at this very minute. Cats are a successful part of that process and have been successful on their own terms.

There have been very few periods in the past six hundred million years when evolutionary changes have been chaotically intense but today is one of them. The first creatures that crawled out of the sea stimulated a burst of evolutionary change. So too did the event that led to the end of the era of dinosaurs. Today's frenzy of evolutionary change is man-made. Bacteria change their behaviour under the influence of antibiotics. Fruit flies change basic genetic structures in their enzyme systems under the influence of insecticides. Moths change their colours from light to dark as soot builds up in industrial England and now change back from dark to light as the Clean Air Act and building restoration eliminates their temporary need for camouflage. All of these evolutionary survival adaptations are caused by the influence of people on the world's environment. And the behaviour of cats is no exception.

By tying itself to people, the domestic cat has become the most successful feline in the history of life on earth. Its alliance with people has given it the freedom to roam all continents and major islands, bar Antarctica. Freedom has come from its alliance with people. To 'liberate' the cat would lead to its inevitable decline.

55. *Humans are hunters. Why don't they understand that I do it just for kicks too?*

This is so obvious that it is puzzling why so many people fail to understand the joy cats get from the hunt, and the fact that the meal is often of secondary importance.

Men who hunt give spurious explanations for their behaviour. They say it is 'traditional', or a chance to 'be with the boys'. Only the most honest admit to the adrenalin surge experienced when they find an animal's fresh trail, sight it and kill it. They don't behave this way to fill the empty stomachs of their family, they hunt because people still carry within them a genetic *need* to hunt.

People who 'hunt' with cameras are also familiar with the physiological rewards of the 'kill'. They too understand the kick they get when the animal is in sight and is shot on film. Twitchers, people who travel the world sighting as many species of birds as possible, are a good example of a selective group of modern hunters.

The adrenalin charge of a successful stalk and capture is not restricted to people who stalk animals; antique hunters get a similar thrill. Just seeing an antique market boosts their adrenalin. And finding a rare item is as great a thrill for the antique hunter as killing Bambi is for the deer hunter – the rewards are similar. Cats hunt for the same reasons; chemical changes in the cat's body produce the same rewards for them as the similar chemical changes that people experience when they hunt for bargains in the Christmas sales.

56. *Why do they think I never swim?*

Cats certainly do swim but most avoid doing so unless it is absolutely necessary. When confronted with water all cats can perform a graceful, but somewhat intense, doggy paddle.

Larger cats swim regularly. The North American Lynx willingly swims broad rivers, as does the African lion. Tigers and jaguars also swim strongly and regularly. The relatively small and quite tamable Fishing Cat of the Indian subcontinent, *Felis viverrinus*, lives on river banks eating birds and small mammals but also frogs and fish. Some have been seen diving for food. The Flat-headed Cat of Malaysia, Thailand, Borneo and Sarawak, *Felis planiceps*, has a similar diet.

The only domestic cat with a natural propensity to swim is the Turkish Van Cat from the Lake Van region of eastern Turkey. In the 1950s, a British traveller, Laura Lushington, observed some unusually long-coated white cats with auburn markings while travelling through eastern Turkey. She noticed these cats had a curious affinity to water. Even adult cats dabbled their feet in pools of water, and cats of all ages swam in the cold waters of Lake Van. During the following years she made several return journeys to the region, selecting cats to bring back to Britain. These formed the root stock of the breed in the West which received formal recognition in 1969.

Few of the descendants of these cats have the opportunity to swim, and with diminishing opportunities have come diminishing desires. As selective breeding continues to favour coat length and colour over behaviour, it is likely that this breed's willingness to do doggy paddle will become as infrequent as it is in other cats.

57. *Why do they get so upset when I stalk and attack them?*

Because people fail to understand that this happens when there is no other prey to stalk.

Hunting is a profoundly basic need for all cats. Good zoos introduce clockwork furries into perspex tunnels in their cat enclosures. The cat sees the furry creature racing through the perspex tube and if it 'captures' the piece of synthetic fur it gets rewarded with a real meal. This keeps captive cats mentally alert.

In large colonies of cats where there is no real prey, the colony selects one or more of the least self-confident members and turns them into pariahs. These cats are physically harassed. The cat behaviourist Paul Leyhausen described how the pariah in his colony was not allowed down from its high perch. It even had to urinate and defecate from it. The British zoologist Jeremy Angel, resident in Japan for over twenty-five years, has written about a colony of over 120 cats that fell under his aegis. He wrote that the timid cats, by running away from confrontations, became the prey substitutes for the rest of the colony. They were so frequently attacked that they left their refuges only when all the others were sleeping.

Stalking and attacking can be signs of dominance but form part of the behaviour of all cats. In Jeremy Angel's colony, the cats that most frequently attacked the pariahs were the middle ranking toms (although higher ranking toms and females also carried out attacks). In people's vermin-free homes, the only movement that some cats ever see are the legs of their owners. In the absence of anything else to hunt these become rodent and bird substitutes. Observant people notice a sudden 'hard' look in their cat's eyes. The cat hides behind furniture, furtively moving from one 'hide' to another. At its chosen time it launches itself at its owner's ankle, sometimes accompanied by a banshee wail. It sinks its teeth in, gives a death bite, then races off.

More often than not it then returns to its site of attack as if nothing has happened. It may even ask for affection or for food. People hate this behaviour but should understand that it is really a sign of frustration. In these circumstances they can diminish repeat episodes by ensuring that the cat has a more productive outlet for its hunting instincts.

58. *Why do vets always frighten me?*

People see vets in a different way from cats. To people, the vet is the animal doctor, someone who is trained in the prevention and treatment of illness and disease. The vet is someone who enhances both the length and the quality of a cat's life. Most vets are gentle with cats. They really like cats. People see this and appreciate it.

Cats see vets in a different way. They are frightening because they are strangers, they dress funny, they are surrounded by unfamiliar smells, they handle cats in ways that only intimates are permitted to do and they cause pain.

In cat terms, a visit to the vet begins with the cat being stuffed in a carrying cage. From experience many cats know that the cage symbolizes anxiety – either the cattery or the vet. This is followed by a car journey. Few cats travel in cars, taxis or public transport with great regularity. Travel is traumatic. Some urinate or defecate with worry.

At the veterinary clinic, the cat, incarcerated in a cage from which it cannot escape, is exposed to the sights and sounds of other strange cats. Some vets have separate dog and cat reception rooms but most cats must suffer the fear and indignity of a strange dog's face peering into its cage from only feet away. After this torment, the cat is transferred to a brightly lit room, its travel box is opened and strange hands reach in and grab it. These hands may be gentle but they are unfamiliar. They open the mouth, widen the eyes, and squeeze the belly. They lift the tail and may insert hard glass or plastic into the rectum. They hold sharp instruments and frequently stab these instruments into the cat squirting cold, sometimes irritating, liquids under the skin or into muscles. They may open the cat's mouth and drop something hard into it, then shut the mouth and make the cat swallow.

People should remember that cats do not know that these torments are for their own wellbeing. So should veterinarians.

59. *Will my image ever improve?*

Yes. It has already.

For over a thousand years the cat has had a serious image problem. In Christian countries the cat has been associated with witchcraft and devil worship. While only four per cent of people in Europe and North America actively hate dogs, over five times as many, just over twenty per cent, actively hate cats. This is now changing and it is changing rapidly.

For centuries cats have been thought of as selfish, self-centred and deceitful. But increasingly they are being thought of as attractive, sensuous, reliable, playful, dependent and chic. This change is occurring quickly because it has emanated from Britain and North America, the world's focal points in pet trends.

None of the historical breeds of cats were developed in Christian countries. But today, more breeds are emanating from Britain and North America than from any regions in the history of the species. Cats are the pets of the future in these countries. They are socially and culturally acceptable, especially if they are expensive purebreds: Ragdolls, Bombays, American Wirehairs, Snowshoes, Tiffanys, Maine Coons, Javanese, American Curls and Ocicats all from the United States; Somalis, Sphynxes and Cymrics from Canada; Javanese, Burmillas, Havana Browns, Devon Rexes, Scottish Folds and Manxes all from Britain.

People have a habit of treasuring their possessions more if the possessions have a high financial value. This has happened to dogs as mongrels have declined, to be replaced by more expensive purebreds. It is now happening with cats. Cats fit into modern Western lifestyles but they have also become fashion statements. Both changes have improved their image and augur well for their future.

60. *I'm planning on emigrating. What is the best country to live in?*

It depends on what a cat is interested in. Some countries, such as Sweden, have advanced cat protection laws. In others, like Switzerland, cats are so well 'protected' that it is illegal to leave them outdoors overnight. Great Britain has excellent humane welfare laws, almost as good as the Nordic countries, but curiously the cat is not included in any legislation that pertains to 'domesticated' animals. People are responsible for the actions of their dogs, horses, sheep, pigs and cattle, but not for their cats.

Some countries have arbitrary laws restricting the movement of cats. In Norway cats must remain within 100 metres of their home. In parts of the State of Victoria, Australia, cats must return home at sunset and remain at home until dawn.

For at least half a century, usually under the influence of bird-loving organizations, governments have attempted to pass legislation to restrict the movement of cats. For example, in 1949, the Illinois State Senate passed a law restricting cats to their owner's property. The State Governor, Adlai Stevenson, vetoed that law and wrote to the Senate, 'I cannot agree that it should be declared policy of Illinois that a cat, visiting a neighbour's yard, or crossing the highway, is a public nuisance. It is the nature of cats to do a certain amount of unescorted roaming . . . to escort a cat abroad on a leash is against the nature of the *owner*.'

Governor Stevenson was not the first to defend the freedom of movement of cats. In *The Origin of the Species*, Charles Darwin, describing how the introduction of one species has a snowball effect on the environment, explained how the introduction of cats into England increased the intensity and variety of wildflowers: cats ate mice, more bumblebees survived mice predation and more flowers were fertilized.

Cat ownership varies considerably from country to country. Here is a list of countries with the percentages of cat-owning homes in each one.

Poland 33%
Australia 32%
United States . . . 31%
Austria 26%
Switzerland . . . 26%
Belgium 25%
France 25%
Canada 24%
Netherlands . . . 24%
Hungary 22%
Italy 22%
Slovenia 22%
United Kingdom . . 22%
Ireland 20%
Sweden 19%
Croatia 18%

Finland	18%
Norway	18%
Denmark	17%
Czech Republic . . .	16%
Slovakia	16%
Portugal	14%
Germany	9%
Spain	8%
Greece	7%
Japan	6%

These figures are for owned cats. If a cat prefers a feral existence, it should choose a temperate climate with an ample food
resource. For these cats the Mediterranean basin remains feline
heaven.

CHAPTER FOUR

The Hidden Health of Cat Owners and Cats

61. *I never go out, ever. I never visit catteries and I hate other cats, passionately. So why do my people have the vet stick needles in me each year?*

People still think of cats as cats used to be; outdoor animals that live by their wits, at risk from infectious diseases acquired through contact with other cats. Under these circumstances routine inoculation to protect against transmissible, often lethal, infections is the best preventative procedure that people can provide for cats. But in the case of cats that never, ever meet other cats the concept of yearly revaccination needs to be thought again.

It is only a single human generation since a viral form of gastroenteritis was a common killer of cats. Routine preventative inoculation against this disease has made it a rarity in pet cats – a real success story. So too with flu viruses; flu was a considerable problem, even among the most expensive pedigree cats from the most sophisticated catteries, until flu vaccines became readily available. Flu is still a major problem in feral cats and a common cause of death in kittens that contract the infection from their mothers.

The leukaemia virus was, and still is, a lethal infection. Mothers can pass this virus on to their litters around the time of birth or it is picked up from the saliva of infected cats during fights. At one time this was a distressingly common and fatal disease in pedigree cats. Breeders now have their breeding stock blood tested and vaccinated against leukaemia and they have been remarkably successful. The disease is now most common among unvaccinated feral cats, spread through bites. This is why it is more common in males, who fight more often, than females.

Vaccination is a success story. Any cat that goes outdoors should have its immunity maintained through reinoculation. Isolated indoor cats live in a uniquely new environment. Those that never meet their own kind, and who live with people who never have close contact with other cats, live in a cat-disease-free environment. Their protection against serious infectious disease will drop, even disappear, with time, but their risk of contact is exceedingly small. It is impossible, however, to anticipate the unexpected; the need for a cat suddenly to stay in a cattery or to be hospitalized. This is a realistic reason for routine revaccinations.

It is at least theoretically possible, however, that by blanket revaccination of all cats vets are not erring 'on the safe side' but rather contributing to other problems. As veterinary medicine has become more sophisticated, the diagnosis of disorders of the immune system has increased. No one knows whether there is a true increased incidence or whether vets are just better at making this difficult diagnosis. If there is a genuine increase in 'immune incompetence' diseases, some feel this may be related to the frequent provocation of the immune system caused by the injection of 'multivalent' vaccines, vaccines that protect against many diseases through one small injection. There is certainly an increased occurrence of a rare skin cancer in the neck region of cats and this cancer has been associated with frequent injections at that site.

Cats do benefit from routine medical examinations. Whether a booster inoculation is included is a matter for the vet, the cat and the owner to ponder.

62. *Why won't my owner touch me. Is it because she's pregnant?*

Yes. She thinks she'll pick up a disease from a cat that may damage her unborn baby. She may be right.

An organism called toxoplasmosis can survive in the muscles of most animals. It is spread from one animal to another when the toxoplasmosis carrier is eaten. The most common way that both cats and people contract this disease is by eating raw or undercooked meat: people eat rare beef; cats eat birds and mice. The organism survives and passes from one animal to another.

About one third of the human population has been exposed to toxoplasmosis and has developed protection against the disease. Some people, usually those with immune systems that do not work well, like hay fever suffers, fail to produce protection when exposed to toxoplasmosis and come down with clinical disease. Unborn babies are most at risk. In Britain about 1,400 pregnant mothers are exposed to toxoplasmosis every year, and many of their babies are born with faulty immune systems. About fifty babies each year have serious vision impairment, even blindness.

Toxoplasmosis has a simple survival trick that makes the cat a potential health hazard to people. The first time, and only the first time, that a cat eats prey that carries toxoplasmosis, the organism is excreted in the cat's faeces for about three to four weeks. Cattle contract the disease by eating feed contaminated by toxoplasmosis laden cat faeces. The organism resides in cows' muscles, which is why pregnant women should not eat undercooked meat and should wear kitchen gloves when preparing raw meat.

Indoor cats are usually not a health hazard to people because they do not have access to wildlife. Cats that do eat wildlife pass toxoplasmosis organisms in their faeces in gardens, contaminating the soil. This is why cats should be prevented from using children's sandboxes as toilets and why pregnant women should always wear impermeable gloves while gardening.

Rather that fret, women should be blood-tested for toxoplasmosis before pregnancy. If they are positive there is no worry; contact occurred in the past. Women who are toxo negative should take precautions, being careful with uncooked meat and in the garden. If they live with outdoor cats they should wear gloves when cleaning the litter tray and wash their hands after having feline cuddles.

63. *I hear all sorts of stories about my effect on people's health. Is their health better or worse with me around?*

There is no definite answer to that question. In an Australian study involving 6,000 households, cat owners attended the doctor twelve per cent less frequently over a year than people who did not have pets. They needed less medication to treat high blood pressure, high cholesterol, heart problems and sleeping difficulties. It is assumed they had a lower incidence of these problems.

Dog owners in Europe and North America certainly appear to have fewer minor health problems, but studies so far do not show the same benefits for cat owners.

The first good examination of the effects of pet ownership on human health was carried out at Cambridge University in England, the most recent by the University of California. Social scientists asked people about their general health before they acquired a cat, immediately after acquiring the cat and then throughout the following year. They asked the same questions of dog owners.

People completed a 'General Health Questionnaire', a well used and approved survey method that measures the incidence of minor health problems. This list included:

headaches
hay fever
sleeping difficulties
constipation
eye problems
bad back
nerves
colds and flu

general tiredness
kidney and bladder trouble
painful joints
trouble with the feet
difficulty concentrating
palpitations and breathlessness
ear problems
worrying over every little thing
indigestion and stomach trouble
sinus and catarrh problems
persistent cough
faints and dizziness

Scientists who conduct these surveys know that there is always a seasonal incidence of minor health problems and, using statistical methods, it is possible to eliminate these blips. When they looked at the results they saw that people reported a significant reduction in minor health problems a month after acquiring a kitten or pup. At six months, this improvement was no longer evident in cat owners. The incidence of minor health problems had reverted to its previous level. (In dog owners the improvement was constant, still there a year after acquiring the pup, when the survey concluded. Using the statistics from the survey, if the incidence of minor health problems was '4' before the survey began, among dog owners it dropped to '2' and remained there.)

The Californian scientists repeated this study and got the same results. It seems, then, that a new kitten in a home has only a transient value in reducing minor health problems in people while a new puppy has long-term value. The initial improvement in human health is probably related to the novelty value of the new pet. People pay less attention to their aches and pains because they are preoccupied by the new and exciting changes. This beneficial effect soon wears off. Dog owners are likely to increase their physical exercise after getting a pup while cat owners do not. It is probably this increase in exercise that accounts for the continuing reduction in minor health problems in dog owners. (The California study showed no improvement in minor health problems for people getting new dogs when they already had a dog. Apparently the health benefits are not magnified with each new canine arrival.)

Nevertheless, the Australian study shows Australian cat owners need fewer medical visits and fewer prescriptions for certain drugs. There seem to be specific health benefits in cat ownership but these are not necessarily the same as the benefits dog owners get from canine companionship.

64. *Does this mean fewer heart attacks for people? Can I really prevent them?*

The scientific evidence here is sound and repeatable. People with cats have lower blood pressure and, if they have heart attacks, they are more likely to be alive a year later than people who don't own cats. Survivability is not related to the severity of the heart attack nor the person's age, sex, financial worth or psychological profile, although it is related to social support. It is not related to personality type. Extensive studies in England show that so-called 'Type A' personalities, with high-risk life-styles, are just as common among cat owners as dog owners or people who don't own pets. In fact, in the largest study, in Coventry, Type A personalities were more likely to own pets.

There is more. Independent scientists questioned the first published reports in the 1980s that connected pet ownership to an increased likelihood of being alive a year after having a heart attack. In the early 1990s, sceptical Australian cardiologists conducted a major survey of over 5,500 people attending a cardiovascular disease risk clinic in Melbourne looking for any relationship between dogs and cats and the risk of heart attacks.

At this clinic patients completed a questionnaire on their eating, exercise and smoking habits. They were weighed and the amount of fat in their body was calculated. They answered questions about their personal and family history of heart disease, their blood pressure was measured and a blood sample was taken for plasma triglyceride and cholesterol measurements. All of these factors are known to be related to increased or decreased risk of cardiovascular disease. In this study, after these routines had been completed, the cardiologists added a final question about pet ownership.

When the results were analysed they revealed that male

cat-owners had significantly lower plasma triglyceride and plasma cholesterol levels than non-cat owners and also slightly, but significantly, lower systolic blood pressure. Female cat-owners aged between forty and forty-nine had significantly lower systolic blood pressure than women who did not own cats. They also had lower plasma triglyceride levels. (Heart disease is the major cause of death in women of this age group in Australia and other countries.) The same beneficial results were seen in dog owners.

The results were unexpected because the scientists set out to show that cat ownership was *not* related to a reduced risk of heart disease. So, they went back and looked for other reasons to explain the reduced risk of heart attacks in pet owners.

There were no differences in body-mass indexes between pet owners and non-pet owners. Their smoking habits were similar but pet owners reported that they ate more take-away food and drank more alcohol than non-pet owners. Pet owners also ate more meat. All of these are factors that increase the risk of cardiovascular disease, not decrease it. Both groups had similar salt and egg consumption. Dog owners did take more exercise but, significantly, cat owners did not. It seems that the reduced risk of heart disease is due to some factors unrelated to exercise.

The social and financial backgrounds of these two groups were similar, as was their level of education. In fact, all of these factors were similar to the Australian national average. (Non-pet owners had marginally higher incomes and slightly more – two per cent more – had completed tertiary or university education.)

Cardiologists know that a drop of one per cent in cholesterol level is associated with a twofold reduction in the risk of death from cardiovascular disease. In this study the cholesterol level in pet owners was two per cent lower than in non-pet owners. (The triglyceride level was thirteen per cent lower in pet owners.) And while the difference in blood pressure was only slight, from the aspect of reducing the risk of heart attack it is substantial and surprisingly similar to another independent study in the United States.

In the United States, people were randomly selected from patients in a nationwide cardiac arrhythmia suppression trial. The researchers observed that cat owners were significantly less likely to die during the year following treatment than non-cat owners. The Americans calculated a three per cent reduction in the probability of death from a heart attack, surprisingly similar to the Australians' calculation of a four per cent reduction. In the United States alone this means 30,000 fewer deaths each year.

The cardiologists concluded, with some reluctance, that there is a relationship between pet ownership and reduced risk factors for heart disease, including reduced blood pressure. Of course, there is no evidence that a cat is the *cause* of this healthy finding, it is still a classic example of the chicken and the egg. Which came first, the cat leading to reduced cardiac-disease risk factors, or a personality profile associated with reduced cardiac-disease risk factors but also with a tendency to keep pets? Who knows?

65. *From the evidence that is available, will people live longer if they live with me?*

There is no evidence that people do live longer. If cats secretly affect the health of people it is through the quality of life and a feeling of well being. There is no evidence, certainly not yet, that quantity is affected. If there were evidence, life insurance companies would find it before anyone else and offer reduced premiums for cat owners. Let me give some examples of how quality, rather than quantity, is affected.

Social scientists in Europe and North America have noted that introducing calm, relaxed cats into nursing homes has a positive effect on residents, especially those who are bed-ridden. In one American study Alzheimer's patients smiled more, touched more and used more words when a cat was placed on their bed. In another Australian study elderly residents in nursing homes showed less confusion, depression, fatigue and tension, and showed more vigour after resident cats were introduced. (The downside was that staff began to use access to the cat as the carrot-on-a-stick to get patients to comply with their demands.) In a Canadian study in Ontario, elderly cat carers were more likely to be able to perform routine daily activities than non-pet owners. These improvements remained as long as the cats lived in the nursing homes.

Similar advantageous changes have been reported so many times from so many countries, involving so many different groups of people in such a variety of institutions that it is no longer news. International scientific meetings are held every few years for people to share their knowledge and information on how cats improve the quality of life.

A common theme emerges from these scientific meetings: people have important needs, such as security and exercise, and slightly less important needs like possessions and sexual activity.

Their most important needs are food and warmth but, just as important, in its own way, is companionship: 'My ears strain to hear. My wits are slow. I spill my food. I repeat my stories. And I breathe happiness when you visit.' Cats are good for people's health because cats offer companionship. The cat's presence is assured, simple and enduring. Its being there simply makes people feel more content. Cat owners do not live longer, but the constancy of cats, the always changing but never changing aspect of their Peter-Pan lives, caught between nature and culture in a state of perpetual innocence and dependence, acts as a rock in some people's lives. Life does not last longer but it is filled with more contentment.

66. *And what about me. I hear I'm a health hazard to people but are people a health hazard to me?*

Critically so. After all, people drive cars and cars kill more cats than any natural predators. People use weapons and shoot cats, either by intention or by accident. People neglect cats but hide that fact from others. But most importantly, people are lethal to all cats because they have the right to make life and death decisions, to decide whether a cat survives or dies.

Cats are destroyed because they are no longer kittens. Stupid people forget that cuddly balls of fluff grow up. Cats are destroyed because they urinate or defecate on carpets or flower beds. People blame their cats, forgetting that the cat's behaviour is 'normal' for cats, but socially unacceptable for people. Rather than go to the bother of changing their own routines or training their cat in order to eliminate the behaviour, they pass death sentences on cats because it is so easy to do. People's personal relationships change and cats die. People move and cats die. No cat has a say in the matter if circumstances have left it in the hands of unthinking, uncaring people.

When a cat becomes elderly a death sentence can still be given, but it will usually be out of love. People ask for death sentences to be carried out on their cats because they feel it is the 'humane thing to do'. This is not necessarily so. With advancing years, cats develop behavioural and mental changes similar to Alzheimer's disease in people. In one study of cats in their teens, almost half of them exhibited at least eleven manifestations of deteriorating mental functions including activity, attention, awareness, hearing and housetraining. Curiously, people were more concerned if their cats were sleeping more or showed reduced activity and attention when they played with their cats, than if they were showing disturbances in house-training. It seems that people are more tolerant of toileting problems in ageing cats than they are of similar problems in ageing humans, a common 'last straw' that leads to the nursing home for elderly people.

Cats often are killed when these senile changes occur because owners feel that their cats are suffering. They forget that, just like people with Alzheimer's, friends and relatives suffer more than the patient. They remember how that person once was and are pained to see such ravaging deterioration. But in advanced senility the patient cannot remember how things once were. So it is with cats. Surprisingly, some of these age-related changes can be arrested, even reversed. Writing in the *British Journal of Psychiatry*, a psychiatrist reported how she responded to senile changes in an elderly cat she inherited as she would with an elderly human. She stroked and groomed the cat more, hand fed it, talked to it frequently and offered it mental stimulation, gentle activity and games. The senile cat responded by becoming more active, gaining weight and demanding food. It seems that the health hazard of death by euthanasia for humane reasons can sometimes be postponed with a little common sense.

67. *Why can't they understand that it's not the nerve gas I object to, it's the cat-like hiss from the aerosol they use?*

Recently, most flea spray manufacturers have realized that this is a problem. They have reduced the sound of the hiss while continuing to use their toxic chemicals.

People hate fleas. It's pathological. They hate them so much they will go to dangerous extremes to keep them out of their homes. Curiously, although people will take great care to feed their cats nutritious food and to prevent contagious disease by vaccinating their cats against dangerous illnesses, they are, unwittingly, willing to cover cats in poisonous nerve gas. Some even make their cats swallow it. (They do it to sheep too, dipping them in it, and while doctors and government officials recognize that farmers who use nerve gas on livestock are themselves at risk, so far there has not been much thought for the sheep.)

Using nerve gas is unnecessary because there are gentler methods to prevent fleas from taking up residence on cats (and people), and gentler methods of eliminating them once they have arrived.

Prevention, as always, is easier, cheaper and safer than cure. And the best way to prevent fleas is to use a biological product, on both cats and their environment, that prevents fleas from reproducing. Biological products do not contaminate the cat with potentially harmful chemicals, they can be used in the cat's environment, on carpets and the cat's bedding. Certain sprays prevent existing flea eggs from hatching and other products can be given as pills. These don't kill fleas but when a flea has a meal on the cat, effectively it swallows flea birth control. It can't reproduce and so it dies off. Because most cats don't mind the odd flea bite, this is a very effective way to get rid of these pests.

For cats that are sensitive to fleas, other safer, non-nerve gas products are available as sprays or shampoos. Any flea that hops on to a treated cat commits suicide. People are edgy about fleas because of a little historical baggage; after all, it was the rat flea that spread bubonic plague throughout Europe. While cat fleas can be irritating to people and even cause allergic reactions in some, there is scant evidence that they transmit serious diseases to people.

68. *I've got this split personality. Do you think that science will ever cure it?*

People say that cats have split personalities but that is, once more, a human perception. What they see as a split personality is simply the range of emotions that cats have.

Cats are in evolutionary transition. Part of their evolution is natural in that it was initiated by cats; they chose to move into human settlements when these new ecological niches developed. This was a wise choice, for it allowed cats to travel in human company as people spread throughout the world. Natural evolutionary pressures selected in favour of cats that were less fearful, and calmer in the presence of people or domesticated animals. The cat's naturally 'wild' temperament was mellowed by self-serving selection for a diffident but cool-headed approach to people and their environment.

More recently people began to intervene in cat breeding, to use the science of genetics. Because people's knowledge of genetics is so basic and primitive, it is unlikely that science will have a dramatic effect on the cat's personality in the near future. All people can do right now is breed selectively for coat length or colour and minor personality characteristics like vocalizing. The distant future is different. Within a few years the human genone, or genetic code, will be completely mapped. Perhaps eighty-five to ninety per cent of that map will be similar in cats. That means that mapping the feline genetic code will be easier, for large parts of it will be identical to that of people. Once the cat's genetic map is available, scientists will have fewer ethical worries about playing with it than they do about playing with human genetics. No doubt cat gene sequences will be manipulated to see what effects those changes have on personality.

69. *Can I ever be sure that human intervention in my breeding will be in my best interest?*

With unfortunate certainty, people will not place the cat's well-being as their highest priority in selective breeding. Some people will always breed cats for reasons of human vanity.

This is already happening. Throughout evolution genetic mistakes always occur, but during the process of natural selection these mistakes are weeded out. Inheritors either fail to survive long enough to mate or, if they do mate, they mate with animals that do not carry harmful genes. Dwarfism and hairlessness are two examples. But today, because people are fascinated by the unusual, even the grotesque, cats that have been born with these traits are nurtured through life then intentionally bred back with their parents or with other known carriers of these deleterious states, to convert recessive characteristics into dominant ones. Some people actually do think that cats with swollen joints and shortened long bones are 'charming'. They think it is 'sweet' the way they have to walk with a shuffle and give them the cutsey name 'Munchkins' after the human dwarfs in *The Wizard of Oz*.

Others selectively breed hairless cats for recognition within the cat world and for financial gain, certainly not for the well-being of cats. Again, they give these luckless individuals a unique name, Sphynx, and parade them at cat shows extolling the virtues of their cats' personalities. Even the most stubborn human understands that hairless cats have no insulation against the elements and are prone to a variety of medical conditions because of their hairlessness. They are equally aware that the personality of a cat is not related to the presence or absence of hair. Personality is not dictated by a single gene associated with hairlessness.

Unfortunately, some cat breeders will look at the catastrophes of dog breeding and try to emulate them with cats. In a free society only moral outrage from the majority of people who respect animals will inhibit people from further attempts to produce grotesques through selective breeding.

70. *Why have scientists carried out so many experiments on my relatives?*

Scientists have a natural curiosity about how people and other animals function. Unfortunately, because cats are cheap, small, quiet, controllable and relatively defenceless, they have suffered at the hands of science. Scientists, especially those who are interested in how the brain and nervous system work, have carried out profoundly unpleasant experiments.

Cruel experimental procedures that were carried out on cats only a generation ago are now considered unethical in many countries, including Britain, Germany and all of Scandinavia. In many other countries, including the rest of Western Europe, North America, Australia and New Zealand, strong ethical guidelines are laid down by governments and these guidelines are augmented by ethical committees at universities. These regulations or suggestions have not prevented continuing experiments with cats.

Overwhelmingly, cats are most at risk from scientists in eastern European countries where ethical guidelines either do not exist or, where they do, are blatantly disregarded. In these countries cats do not have a sufficiently large part of the population lobbying on their behalf. But there is one strong ray of hope. Researchers in these countries take pride in the publication of their results in respected international science journals and virtually all of these journals set high ethical standards for any scientific work that they publish. It is in the self interest of scientists to ensure that cats are not needlessly experimented on if they wish to maintain access to these scientific publications.

71. *What is the risk of my being turned into a pair of gloves?*

The risk is low in wealthy Western countries but still high in poor eastern regions of Europe.

It is only a few decades since the bodies of dead cats in Britain and France were completely 'recycled'. Body collectors skinned the carcasses, selling cat pelts by the tens of thousands to Poland, where the fur was used as lining in gloves. The remains were rendered down and used as fertilizer.

This was recycling at its most efficient but, curiously, as the international ecological or 'green' movement has promoted recycling in other areas of human endeavour, it has not encouraged recycling of pet cats. Human emotion interferes with human logic.

In affluent sectors of Western civilization, at the end of the twentieth century people can luxuriate in a feeling of compassion for all living creatures, but only because their bellies are full and their homes warm. Poverty exists in the West but its amplitude is wholly different from that in other parts of the world. Throughout eastern Europe dogs and cats serve more pragmatic purposes than simply companionship. In Russia, cats and dogs are apparently stolen and skinned for their hides. Large white dogs fetch the highest prices from tanners.

Some people love and care for cats not because of any moral or cultural superiority, but because the success of their culture permits them to do so. That is why the cat welfare movement is now gaining support in Japan and Singapore while in eastern European countries animal welfare remains a minority idea. When it comes to cats, affluence and education breed compassion.

72. *Fat, juicy mice make me quiver with excitement. I lust for raw meat. Why do they feed me only crunchy food? Why won't they let me eat what I want?*

In a logical world cats would be fed the world's surplus of meat that people do not want. Misguided political correctness prevents this from happening. In many parts of the world, populations of wild animals are 'culled', a euphemism for 'killed', because of overgrazing or overpopulation leading to increased parasitic problems and other diseases. Seals are culled in Europe, elephants are culled in South Africa, deer are culled in North America and, most numerous of all, kangaroos are culled in Australia.

All of these animals offer superb nutrients for cats, but animal lovers hate the idea of turning these wild animals into cat food. Instead they are burned or buried. It's psychological, there is no logic involved.

This is odd because only a few human generations ago most cats lived off wild animals. The very reason why cats were first permitted to inhabit human settlements was based on their efficiency to kill (and eat) wildlife people did not want to live with – mice and rats.

In the mid-nineteenth century, British manufacturers invented 'dog food'. The first dog food was simply hard seamen's biscuits that had got too maggot infested even for sailors. Though the biscuit was rather tasteless, manufacturers realized there was a market for dog food. They continued to sell hard dog biscuit but also invented tinned foods, made from meat unfit for human consumption. Tinned cat food soon followed.

By the middle of the twentieth century both the sources for cat food and their manufacturing processes had changed.

Reputable manufacturers no longer used products unfit for human consumption. Instead they became efficient 'scavengers', searching for cheap surpluses of food produced for the human food chain. Europe, with its farm subsidies that favoured overproduction, and North America, Australia and New Zealand, with their intensive agricultural industries that produced cheap protein, were constant sources of good-quality protein. Industrial fishing produced fish by-products ideal for cat food. Most of these forms of protein went into tinned food. To cats – and their owners – the food looked like processed meat and smelled like processed meat. Then something strange happened: manufacturers discovered that people were willing to feed their cats dry food out of boxes and cats enjoyed eating it.

This cultural change began in the United States but rapidly spread to Canada and then Europe and beyond. These foods are eaten straight from the box, like biscuits. No one knows why people's attitudes changed but within a decade dehydrated, or dry, cat foods became significant items worldwide. Cats liked them.

Now, cat food manufacturers upped the ante. When they saw there was a sophisticated market demand for high-quality cat

food, some started competing with manufacturers who processed foods for human consumption. Personally, I don't
approve of this change because there is, and there will continue
to be, a surplus of protein available for cat food. Manufacturers
simply have to look for it. By competing with manufacturers of
food for people they just drive up the price of processed food
for human consumption.

A mouse may offer perfect nutrition for a cat but today few
cats survive on that natural diet. They depend upon feline nu-
tritionists for their wellbeing. The world's largest cat-food
manufacturers make certain that all the nutrients a cat needs
are in these foods. And, although they do not look particularly
appetizing to people, they seem to be superbly tasty to most
felines.

73. *Why did they sterilize me without asking? Who gave them the right?*

They did. People assume they have the right to make decisions about all aspects of animal life. Many think it is a divine right, a God-given right.

Cats must face reality. People are the dominant species on this planet, dominant in the sense that their behaviour is more influential than the behaviour of all other animals. It may be that the biomass of ants is greater than the biomass of humans but ants use very few other living things for their own selfish purposes. People have the capacity to denude forests, contaminate the greatest lakes and rivers in the world, breed and kill animals as they wish, alter evolution and sterilize any cats they choose.

I am not saying that this is a bad bargain for cats. In fact it has been an incredibly good bargain. In giving up its right to independence and its right to choose its own mates, the cat has become the most successful of all members of the Feline family, ever. Over two hundred million cats live worldwide. No other feline species, lions, tigers, pumas, lynxes, even sabre-toothed tigers, has been even remotely as successful at being fruitful and multiplying.

The cat and the human parasitize each other but are what scientists call saprophytic parasites; they benefit each other. For the benefit of security, food, comfort and good health, cats have given up the right to procreate according to their own selection processes. People increasingly make the choice for people reasons, not cat reasons. There is no evidence that people, other than a minority fringe who believe that all species of animals should breed according to their own perceptions of the survival of the fittest, will give up this control at any time in the future.

74. *I walk slowly. I can't jump up on the table any longer. And I've got decent people. Why can't they see I'm in pain and do something about it?*

People cry when they hurt. People complain when they are uncomfortable. And they think that because these are their reactions to pain, cats behave the same way when they hurt.

Of course, cats are far more stoic than people. Cats suffer silently unless a pain is sudden and acute, like when someone steps on a cat's tail. Many people fail to read the cat's body language of chronic pain: depending upon where the pain is, a cat will carry its head in a more concentrated way; it might lean forward or arch its back or favour a painful leg by limping; it might no longer spring up from a resting position but get up front first, then drag up its hindquarters; it might find it difficult to lie down and just crash instead of finding an intentional position. Cats with chronic pain in the hindquarters no longer jump with ease while cats with chronic forequarter pain are apprehensive about jumping down.

When cats suffer from chronic pain they approach their affliction the way doctors tell people to contend with their chronic pain. Cats get on with life, they live with their pain. They don't spend their time thinking about the way they used to be. Just as people should do but find it almost impossible to do, a cat takes as its point of reference its period of worst pain. It continues with life and still enjoys food and affection. It does not get morose.

Because cats do not complain even decent, knowledgeable, caring and considerate owners often fail to understand that changes in the cat's rhythm of life have been caused by pain. They often feel that their cat is 'slowing down' because it is 'growing older'. The most observant cat owners see changes in body language and understand that these are associated with pain but even some of these people feel that pain is a regrettable but unavoidable part of ageing.

Sometimes a degree of pain is unavoidable but in the vast majority of instances a cat's chronic pain can be diminished, especially pains associated with ageing. People forget that there have been great advances in pain control for humans and that these advances apply to cats too.

Aspirin and paracetemol are quite dangerous for cats (although aspirin, given in small quantities on a twice-weekly basis may be the treatment of choice for certain blood clot problems). There are a variety of alternative ways to reduce the discomfort of chronic pain for cats; deep heat, ultrasound, acupuncture, massage, even skin patches of slow-release pain killers. The intensity of pain can almost always be diminished but this depends completely upon a cat's owner realizing that his or her uncomplaining cat is in pain in the first place.

75. *I am always itchy. I can't sleep without jumping up and scratching. Can I possibly be allergic to my owners?*

Absolutely. People seldom realize it but they are often the hidden cause of their cat's itchy skin condition. The problem concerns the way people live. Dutch research suggests that as many as twenty per cent of itchy cats are itchy because of the human environment they live in.

In this century, people have created warmer, softer home environments than ever before. Central heating is normal in most countries with a temperate climate. Wall-to-wall carpeting is common in countries such as Great Britain, Canada and the United States. These two facts have led to an explosion in the population of house dust mites and these are a common cause of allergic skin reaction in some cats.

There was a time when the cat slept outdoors or in the kitchen. Not now. People are more intimate with cats and most permit their cats to have access to their bedrooms. But this exposes allergic cats to yet another cause of itchy coats and watery eyes; sloughing human skin – people dander. The two most common indoor allergens that provoke an allergic response in cats are human dander and dust mites that live off human dander (or, to be more accurate, the dust mites' droppings).

The only way cats can avoid these potential irritants is to change their owner's lifestyle. Wall-to-wall carpets, especially in bedrooms, should be abolished and replaced by hard floors. Rugs should be small enough to be cleaned easily. People should allow more fresh air in their homes. They should open their windows to allow wind to drive out some of the suspension of house dust mite droppings that always hangs in the air. Sensible cats should never sleep on their owner's bed. This is a disgusting place. After only a few years virtually one-third of the weight of a person's pillow consists of human dander, dead dust mites and their droppings. It is the same with people's mattresses. Although people are quick to recognize that they can be allergic to cats, it is just as likely that cats are allergic to people.

76. *I hear terrible tales about other cats being abused. What is the risk of my being battered? If I am, will anyone know? Will anyone help?*

Cats, because they are cats, are always at risk of being abused. Often, few people outside the cat's human family know. But if any people know that abuse is taking place there are organizations that will help, including the courts.

People have an almost irrational attitude towards cats. The law defines a cat simply as 'goods' or 'chattels'. Cats are *owned* by people. Because cats are possessions, they are sold, traded or discarded. Legislation exists that prevents cruelty to animals but this usually applies to extreme cruelty, seldom to benign neglect or the occasional kick.

On the other hand, cats are 'members of the family'. People develop an emotional attachment to cats. People understand that cats have feelings and emotions, that they can be distressed, anxious, agitated, happy, joyful or euphoric.

This dichotomy of human attitude, that a cat is a sentient being but also simply a possession, creates problems. A cat can be loved one minute and abused the next. It is treated as a member of the family, fed and cared for, then discarded when the family moves or simply tires of it.

Physical abuse is easy. Cats are small. In a classically cartoon sense, the boss dumps on the employee, the employee goes home and dumps on his son, the son kicks the cat. Everyone wants a scapegoat.

In families where wives and children are abused there is an increased likelihood that cats too are battered. In a study in Utah, three-quarters of battered women reported that their cats were abused. Frighteningly, almost one quarter reported that their own children hurt or killed their cats. Some animal welfare agencies, especially the largest, work in conjunction with social service agencies responsible for monitoring children at risk. Those responsible for child welfare and those responsible for pet welfare should share information with each other. By doing so the risk to women, children and cats might be reduced.

77. *Why do gardeners loathe me?*

As far as gardeners are concerned cats are vermin. They despoil gardens by defecating in the perennials and digging in the borders. They urinate on the hedges. This dislike is universal while it should, in fact, be directed only at specific cats.

Neighbours' cats, often accused of this behaviour, are more likely to make careful incisions in bags of waste and remove cooked chicken carcasses than mess over an extended area. Neutered females usually do little territory marking and are happy to leave all their droppings in one designated site; the litter tray or one spot in the garden. Neutered males may have a hankering to mark out a little more territory but even they are most likely to defecate only in a specific site.

Unwittingly, gardeners prepare their flower beds to the exact texture and consistency preferred by the great territory markers, unneutered tom cats. Given their choice of toileting sites, cats often choose loose, well-turned soil. Dominant male cats leave their droppings uncovered as visible markers of their territory. They leave pungent urine marks on designated sites for the same purpose. Gardeners often accuse a cat-owning neighbour of permitting their cat to despoil the garden. Most owned cats are neutered and produce virtually odourless urine. Powerful urine and unburied faeces are the markers of the dominant feral tom cat, owned by no one, king of his domain. But gardeners rarely see him because he carries out most of his territory marking at dawn, while they frequently see neighbours' neutered cats because they are often out and about while people are gardening.

78. *Will people ever eat me?*

Where possible, cats should avoid Guangdong and other parts of southern China.

Eating cat has historically been a human behaviour only when starvation is at hand. Compared to herbivore meat such as rabbit and hare, cat has a pungent aroma and sharp taste. Cat liver in excess is potentially dangerous to humans.

Cat has never featured on the menu as much as dog has in many parts of the world, but in southern China new-found affluence has brought an upsurge in eating cat as a delicacy. Stray cats are rounded up by cat catchers and sold to restaurants. Diners may choose their cat as lobster eaters choose theirs in European and North American restaurants. The cat is usually battered to death, skinned, then seasoned and cooked. (Lobsters, on the other hand, are simply thrown alive into boiling water.)

Cat owners find it horrific to watch film of scenes in these restaurants (so do I), but their moral grounds for revulsion are questionable if, while being disgusted by those who eat cat, they willingly eat other mammals like cattle, pigs, rabbits or sheep. Of course, few people today keep these animals as household companions and pet animals are placed on a different ethical level from other domesticated animals, but this is based only upon the familiarity people have with them rather than on any innate differences between these and other animals. In their willingness to eat anything that moves, and to disregard any torment that an animal feels, at least the diners of Guangdong are showing a moral consistency. Westerners are morally inconsistent with their treasuring of one species and abuse of another.

CHAPTER FIVE

The Hidden History of Cat Owners

79. *In my family's library I found the most frightening book I have ever seen:* One Hundred and One Uses for a Dead Cat. *How can anyone write a book like that? How can anyone buy it?*

There's no denying it. Few people actively hate dogs (which is why no one has written *One Hundred and One Uses for a Dead Dog*) but lots of people, about one in five, hate cats. Their reasons are partly personal but mostly cultural.

Some cultures just don't like cats. Others do. Cats were disliked in Singapore which is why, in the survival of the fittest, the little Singapura evolved with a faint, soft meow. In nearby Thailand cats were admired, especially by the royal household of Siam. That's why the Siamese evolved with such a strident voice, it had no need to hide.

In Judeo-Christian cultures cats were generally disregarded until about 700 years ago when they became associated with devil worship. Cats in Europe entered an era of persecution from which they are only now emerging. Ritual massacres of cats took place throughout Europe, especially in France. There was a widely held belief that witches, almost always women, could turn themselves into cats and vice versa. This belief crossed the Atlantic to New England where it featured in the Salem witch trials in 1692. In Western societies, culturally speaking, cats have had a pretty poor press.

Not so in Arab cultures. Islamic tradition tells the story of a cat that used to visit Mohammed in the house where he lived. One day, when it was time for prayer, Mohammed saw that the cat had fallen asleep on his garment. Rather than disturb it, he cut off the part the cat was sleeping on and slipped away. Cultural affection for cats in Arab countries has its origins in stories such as this. Maybe that is why *One Hundred and One Uses for a Dead Cat* has never been translated into Arabic.

80. *Why does the Church hate me?*

No one really knows exactly how the association developed but by the twelfth century cats had become associated with European paganism and witchcraft. When the Church embarked upon a centrally organized persecution of heretics it ended up persecuting cats too.

In 1233 Pope Gregory IX declared that heretics worshipped the devil in the form of a cat. That declaration initiated a persecution that persists even today. In the following centuries association with cats was sufficient cause for persecution, torture, imprisonment or death. In the mid-thirteenth century, a revival in Germany of the pagan cult of Freya was suppressed by associating cultists with cats. In the fourteenth century, when Pope Clement V decided to suppress the order of Knights Templar he accused them of homosexuality, but also of worshipping the devil in the form of a cat. By the time bubonic plague spread the black death across Europe, cats had been so vilified by the Church they were accused of being the devil's messengers of death and were hunted out and destroyed, leaving rats free to continue spreading the epidemic.

It is likely that the cat's persecution is a consequence of people simply not understanding why cats behave as they do. Evil spirits, according to the Church, roamed the countryside at night, the time when cats are most active. It took only a little imagination on the part of someone to suggest that cats were active at night not to hunt for mice, but to warn evil spirits to disappear before they could be seen.

In the fifteenth century, Pope Innocent VIII intensified the Church's search for heretics, and for the next four centuries cats became associated with witchcraft. Common belief considered that witches had supernatural accomplices, often in the form of small animals. At that time few people kept pets as companions, so an elderly woman showing affection to or compassion for a cat would certainly have appeared an odd individual to the rest of the community.

Today, people have forgotten the origins of the Church's antipathy towards cats, but for many the cat remains associated with mystery and magic. Crossing the path of a black cat brings bad luck (unless you live in the American Midwest where it brings good luck). In the Deep South of the United States some people still think that if a cat is allowed to sniff a human corpse disaster will fall upon the whole family. Once people develop their beliefs and attitudes they are firmly resistant to change. The Church may no longer actively hate cats but the residue of its animosity to felines will continue in a varied form as popular folk wisdom.

81. *My owner is a politician. Why did he have the dog in the family portrait but not me?*

The politician's attitude is a good example of 'popular folk wisdom' in the United States and France.

For most of this century the image of a man with his wife, children and pet dog has, to image makers, been the accepted recipe for representing stability, security, constancy and fidelity. A man who has a dog is a good man, concerned about his family and the future. The presence of the dog sends the subliminal message that he also cares about his 'extended family'; the voters in his ward, precinct, town, county, state, province or country.

In the United States and France, successive presidents have always had their dogs included in some photographs. Presidents Johnson, Nixon, Ford, Carter, Reagan and especially President Bush used their dogs to symbolize their integrity. President Bush's dog was photographed sleeping by his desk as he made momentous decisions. In France Presidents Giscard, Pompidou, Mitterrand and Chirac have been photographed with their dogs. News stories tell of how Chirac responded when his Labrador died, revealing to his constituents that he is a 'caring and considerate' man. The American Republican Party historically asked its candidates to include their dogs in their family portraits, but candidates were explicitly instructed not to include their cats. According to political image makers, the presence of a cat infers venality, deceit, selfishness, greed, avariciousness, fraudulence and dishonesty.

Political cat antipathy has not existed in Britain in this century but that is probably a legacy of Queen Victoria's admiration of felines. Her favourite cat, White Heather, survived her and continued to live on in Buckingham Palace well into the reign of King Edward VII. A few decades later

Winston Churchill was so attached to his ginger tom, Jock, that it sat in on wartime cabinet meetings and he personally took Jock with him to safety during air raids.

Cats continued to be a feature of 10 Downing Street. When Harold Wilson was Prime Minister and his Siamese, Nemo, was an honorary member of his Cabinet, the Italian Ambassador to Britain was asked what he would like to do if he had his life to live over again. He replied: 'I would like to be a cat in London . . . or a cardinal in my country.' Cats continue to live at 10 Downing Street. The present incumbent, Humphrey, makes newspaper headlines when he vanishes and returns. The subliminal message is that Humphrey has his freedom to live as he wishes. Image makers are fully aware of the value of this message on the British electorate.

Image makers are also aware of the value of Socks, the feline resident of the Clinton White House. Socks receives over 100,000 fan letters each year, all answered by volunteer teams who sign each letter with a paw print. To Republicans, it is politically poetic that President Clinton, viewed by them as a deceitful and dishonest president, has a cat. Some Democrat image makers are concerned about this but others understand the shifting demographics of cat ownership in the United States. For most of this century the dog has been the Americans' favourite pet, but in the late 1980s cat numbers overtook those of dogs for the first time. This trend continues. The number of cat-owning households increases each year while the number of homes with dogs declines. As more voters live with cats you can bet your bottom dollar that the political image of cats is bound to improve. French cats, with greater historical burdens, will have to wait a little longer.

82. *Why do they keep me, an African, as a companion, but not my European relatives?*

It is true that the pet cats of Europe are African immigrants. Although there is an indigenous small cat that once lived throughout all of Europe except Ireland and Scandinavia, and still lives in Scotland, France, Spain, Italy, Germany and throughout central Europe, the resident's personality simply was not and is not amenable to living close to humans.

People have tried to live with the European Wildcat and have failed. This is a secretive feline, a lone hunter that avoids all contact with people. It is slightly larger than a typical pet cat and its hunting prowess has made it the scourge of gamekeepers. Trapping and poisoning drove the Wildcat to the verge of extinction. It was only the wartime need for soldiers that prevented British gamekeepers from finishing their task. Since the Second World War, wildlife legislation has protected the European Wildcat and in Scotland, in particular, it has increased in numbers to a secure level. Competition between wildcats in the depths of the Highlands has driven the boldest on to the fringes of agricultural land where they dine on rabbits. Still, they are rarely seen by people. When kittens are discovered and raised in human families they remain as fierce and untameable as they were a thousand years ago. This cat has never chosen to live near people.

Its close relative, the African Wildcat, did. No one knows when this cat chose to move into human settlements but archeological evidence suggests that this evolutionary change probably occurred over eight thousand years ago. By four thousand years ago, the Egyptians were so familiar with this 'self domesticated' carnivore they made it one of their gods.

The African Wildcat had a malleability of temperament lacking in its European cousin. To get a little technical, it had a more flexible system of internal hormones. Its 'fight or flight' mechanism was more plastic so it was able to remain cool, calm and collected in the presence of people. There may have been only a few individuals with this modified 'biofeedback mechanism' but evolution is profoundly fast in selecting for survival. Calm African Wildcats survived in their new environment, living off the mice attracted to human settlements. People throughout the world keep their descendants as companions today.

83. *Why was I taken out of Africa in the first place?*

African Wildcats did not migrate on their own out of Africa and the Middle East. They were transported by people.

While the Egyptians venerated the now domesticated African Wildcat, other local people disregarded it. In the Old Testament there is only one reference to cats and it is unclear whether the cats (that were to rain on the heads of the Babylonians) are large or small, domestic or wild.

Human curiosity is likely to have been a primary reason for cats leaving Africa. The Greeks were probably curious about an animal venerated by the Egyptians and wanted to see it. Value followed. It was in a trader's financial interest to capture, purchase or steal cats to trade with those who were curious about them. Cats became a commodity. Only much later, when the black rat became a common pest in the holds of ships, did cats become sailors' companions.

84. *How did my relatives end up in Asia, the Americas, Australia, in fact almost everywhere in the world and how did they get there so quickly?*

Once the cat had become a commodity, it was rapidly transported by traders around the world. It first spread to the northern shores of the Mediterranean and, about 2,200 years ago, it reached India and China. Although legend says that cats reached Japan in 999 A.D., they actually arrived on those islands several hundred years earlier, about 1,300 years ago.

A population geneticist, writing in *Scientific American*, has documented how the spread of cats around the world can be traced according to the frequency of coat colours. He described how the frequency of blotched tabby increases along the course of the Rhône River valley, from low frequency at its mouth on the Mediterranean to moderate frequency in the heart of Europe. That frequency increases along the course of the Rhine and Seine rivers as they flow towards the North Sea and English Channel, and reaches its highest in the south of England where it has become the dominant coat pattern.

The first domestic cats to reach North America were taken there only 300 years ago by French explorers to what is now Canada. Some were offered as gifts by missionaries to local Huron Indians but it is doubtful that any survived. Although other domestic cats occasionally arrived in the English, Dutch and French colonies, it was only when a plague of rats infested the colony of Pennsylvania in the 1700s that cats were actively imported. These cats came from southern English ports such as Portsmouth and Bristol. They were predominantly blotched tabbies and their American descendents today reflect the coat colour patterns of cats in southern England 250 years ago. In a similar sense the colour variety of Australian cats reflects coat colour patterns in English port cities 150 years ago.

Cats populated the world not only as a commodity. In the early 1700s, the brown rat invaded Europe. It reached the port of Copenhagen in 1716, English ports by 1729, central Europe by 1753 and northern Scandinavia by 1762. By 1775 it was a pest throughout North America. More robust than the black rat, which was brought back to Europe from Africa by Crusaders, the brown rat easily adapted to life on ships. To control them, most ship owners used resident ship's cats. Wherever European ships travelled, rats and cats followed. And wherever ships were wrecked, rats and cats often survived. This is how cats appeared in such remote and hostile environments as uninhabited Marrion Island in the subantarctic, or in the Galapagos. Intentionally and by accident, people spread cats around the world. The cat's evolutionary success is based upon its own ability to adapt to its surroundings but also on its chance transportation over oceans by people.

85. *I am orange and white. How did I end up on the Norwegian coast when my family is Turkish?*

Blame it on the Vikings or their trading partners. Orange-and-white cats are most common in eastern Turkey, the Turkish Van cat is an excellent example. But across Europe this genetically sex-linked colour is very rare, except in Brittany in northern France, in coastal regions of northern England and Scotland, and in Scandinavia. The only way for orange-and-white cats to have arrived in these regions is by direct transport from Turkey. It is very possible that their ancestors arrived in Norway on Viking longships. The lack of other cats to breed with meant that the original coat colours and patterns have been retained, even today.

86. *I'm a black cat. Why am I relished in one place and feared in the next?*

The black cat has a curious image throughout Europe and North America. In Sicily it represents the Evil Eye. A black cat in the house brings bad luck (Strangely, in Kentucky, a black cat's visit to a house brings good luck, unless it decides to stay, which brings bad luck.) In nineteenth-century Britain a black cat walking in front of a bride and groom was a happy omen while in France the presence of the black cat is an unlucky event.

Sailors once considered it lucky to have a black cat on board ship (but unlucky to say the word 'cat'). Sailors' wives kept black cats to ensure their husbands' safe return. A spinster keeping black cats was deemed unlucky because she risked being labelled a witch.

The colour black is genetically dominant in cats, so it is common. For natural dawn and dusk hunters it is excellent camouflage, which is why it is such a successful colour, but to superstitious Europeans in the Middle Ages the very fact that only its eyes were visible at night and not its body was sufficient for it to be deemed supernatural, the devil in disguise.

Today, black cats have less to worry about. It is a popular colour in many breeds – even the star attraction of one breed, the Bombay, which only comes in shimmering black.

87. *Why do people create different breeds of cat? Isn't the original model good enough?*

Initially people did not create different breeds of cat, natural evolution did. The Siamese, Birmans, Angoras, Persians, Turkish Vans, blues like the Chartreux, Abyssinians, Manx, Japanese Bobtail and others evolved their own shapes, colours and coat textures to cope with the environments in which they lived. The presence of humans was a distinct environmental pressure but evolution occurred without human intervention. For example, in Japanese mythology the devil cat *nekomata* had a bifurcated tail that was the source of its supernatural powers. Cats without tails could never become devil cats so the devil-cat superstition favoured naturally tailless cats. Because Japan remained isolated from the rest of the world for so long, centuries of breeding within a closed cat population probably allowed the tailless condition to become more common, not only because it already existed in the limited gene pool but because people liked these cats, so they were more likely to survive and mate.

More recently, especially in the last fifty years, people have selectively bred cats to create new breeds. More new breeds have been created since 1950 than in the entire preceding 7,000 years of domestic cat breeding. Some of these new breeds are simply the result of selecting for what was already there. The Norwegian and Siberian Forest Cats, and probably the Maine Coon, all are breeds that developed thick and dense coats of coarse guard hair to insulate themselves from the harsh northern environments they found themselves in. Breeders noticed these natural changes and accentuated them through controlled and selective breeding. Other breeds developed because natural genetic mutations were perpetuated. This is how the Rex cats and the Cymric, the long haired Manx, became distinctive breeds.

In other instances, with an excellent understanding of the science of genetics, breeders selectively embark on the production of a new breed, crossing the Burmese with the Chinchilla to create the Burmilla, or the Siamese with the Burmese to create the Tonkinese. A more striking example is the Bengal, created by crossing a domestic cat with a small, wild feline species.

People will continue to create new breeds for the variety of reasons that motivate human endeavour – pride, vanity, financial reward, arrogance, elitism, scientific or cerebral satisfaction, a sense of achievement. In most instances this human endeavour is benign but when the gene pool of a new breed is small, or when obvious defects are selected for, this human propensity can have an enduring deleterious effect on cats.

88. *I'm always matted (and I hate being brushed). Why did they interfere and give me this ridiculous coat?*

Selecting for soft, long coats is a very recent fad. Natural selection for long coats occurred in many different countries. The first longhaired cats to reach Europe were imported from the Ankara region of Turkey. These were rather lithe, long cats with the longest hair on their necks and were called Angoras. Later, cats with denser coats of hair and more compact bodies were imported from Persia. These became Persians.

In their original forms these breeds were probably more like the present day longhaired cats of northern Europe, with longer guard hair and denser insulating down. With the advent of cat shows and the development of breed standards, their naturally long coats took a turn for the worse. The Persian, for example, was to have as soft a coat as possible. This impelled breeders to select more and more for soft, thin, downy hair rather than the coarser but more self-cleaning guard hair. The result is an unnatural coat, one that needs daily attention from people to prevent it from matting, attention that many Persians would rather not have.

89. *I want to be secure. What country should I emigrate to?*

People have different plans for cats in different parts of the world so this depends upon how cats will be treated. Cats wanting independence should choose different countries, or regions within countries, from their jailed relatives.

In a country such as Australia, where many people feel that the cat is a threat to native fauna, it is likely that an increasing part of the population, sensitized to the ecological effects that introduced species have, will be wary of more free-roaming domestic cats. Independent cats could choose a better country to live in.

In small countries such as Britain, although cat numbers are increasing, independent cats face a similar insecurity. Bird protection groups are numerous and articulate in their charge that domestic cats are decimating Britain's songbirds. Gardeners have a similarly powerful lobby, accusing cats of spreading disease and havoc in their gardens. (In reality the 'bird murderer' charge bears little substance. Although total cat numbers have increased in Britain, the actual number of outdoor cats has remained relatively constant for a considerable time. The increase in the cat population is mostly an increase in the incarcerated indoor cat population.)

The United States, and to a lesser extent Canada, remain the ideal destination countries for cats planning to migrate, and for several reasons. North America already has an immense variety of small, land-based carnivores. Increasing numbers of free-roaming cats endanger no domestic wildlife to the point of extinction as, at least in theory, they may do in Australia and New Zealand. Canada should only be chosen by independent cats that enjoy sharp seasonal changes; Mediterranean summers and Arctic winters.

Americans have many plans in mind for cats, most of which are in the cat's interest. In the United States, cat numbers increase yearly and will continue to do so. An ageing human population is in the cat's interest. Dog numbers will continue to decline (and the average size of dogs will shrink), while cat numbers will increase as more people find themselves feeling alone, even in the middle of cities, and in need of companionship. California is probably the best state to live in, although Texas is also appealing. There are more cat-loving organizations there than perhaps anywhere else in the world. Cat lovers are as numerous as bird lovers. Cat lovers ensure continuing progress in veterinary medicine, discoveries that reduce the incidence of cat diseases and improve the quality of cat life. (Cats should be aware, however, that some of these cat lovers make such a high emotional investment in their cats that they are unwilling to 'let go' when a cat has reached the end of its natural existence, and demand that veterinarians keep a cat alive when it really is not in the cat's interest.)

There is one other unexpected country that may be worth investigating and that is Japan. The cat's history in Japan is varied. For hundreds of years after its introduction, the cat was the plaything of aristocrats and cats were kept on leashes until the 1700s when they were released, to attack the mice infesting the silkworm industry. Cats have never been institutionally hated in Japan as they were in Europe. Indeed, for most of Japan's history cats were respected. Only in the last 200 years have they faced indifference. This may change in the future.

Today's generation of urban Japanese has successfully incorporated dog ownership into its lifestyle. It may have done so initially because it was a manifestation of Western culture, but dog ownership is now a firm part of urban Japanese culture. The same change is occurring with cat ownership, and specifically with pedigree cat ownership. Urban Japanese have discovered the pleasures but also the inconvenience of dog ownership. It is only a matter of time before they dip into cat ownership, as happened in Western Europe and North America only a generation ago. Just as cats are the most popular domestic pets in the United States, Britain and Canada, so too in the future they will be the most popular pets in Japan.

90. *Will there be more cats in the future?*

Yes. People have ensured that cat numbers will continue to increase. Variety will increase as well.

The future of cats is ensured because cats are so adaptable. In an evolutionary sense, their numbers are so great that threats to their future are met by adaptations by only a few that then spread throughout the population. The cat adapted from the life of a solitary hunter to that of a hunter and scavenger willing to live in close proximity to people. It adapted from life in tropical and semi-tropical climates to survival in temperate and even Arctic conditions. It adapted from a life of total independence to one of willing dependency. The cat is one of evolution's great success stories but its greatest success, like the rat's, has been its association with people.

That association will continue. People will take their cats with them wherever they go. Only Antarctica will remain a forbidden land for cats. People will continue to interfere with natural feline evolution by selectively breeding cats for traits that people desire. Because cats are neat, quiet, self-cleaning, self-sufficient, dignified but, most importantly, physically alluring, people will make sure their numbers continue to increase.

91. *In the future will people make us bigger or smaller?*

Both of these changes will occur.

Ten thousand years ago, dogs were all the size of Asian wolves, weighing about twenty-five kilograms. Through selective breeding dogs today range from one to one hundred kilograms. This shrinkage and enlargement was possible because the genetic potential already existed within the extended Canine family, from the tiny Fennec fox to the massive Canadian Timber wolf.

Such a genetic plasticity does not exist within the Feline family but there is still considerable room for shrinking and enlarging the domestic cat. The pet cat's close 'wildcat' relatives vary from the thirty-seven-centimetre long Black-footed cat of the Kruger National Park in South Africa, to the ninety-four-centimetre long Chinese Desert cat of Central Asia. This means there is the genetic plasticity within the domestic cat to shrink or enlarge within these parameters. Breeders will, without doubt, attempt these changes.

For better or worse, genetic engineering will also influence the size of future cats. Scientists will continue to find cats easy subjects to experiment on. They will discover genes that appear to control growth and growth rates in one species of cat and splice the genes into another to see what happens. Ethics committees will have difficulty preventing experiments such as these from happening.

92. *Will scientific breeding tear my soul apart?*

This is a great moral dilemma facing medical science. Virtually all of the scientific breakthroughs in the advancement of people's understanding of genetics have taken place using animals: artificial insemination was developed in livestock; freezing sperm and inseminating females long after the male had died was developed in agricultural animals; harvesting eggs from one female, fertilizing them in a test tube then implanting the fertilized egg in another female was originally a veterinary technique; freezing eggs then thawing them years later and fertilizing them was another veterinary procedure. Moral considerations only developed when these techniques were applied to people.

The same situation exists with genetic engineering. Through genetic manipulation a sheep is crossed with a different species, the goat, to create a new species, the geep. Some people are concerned, but bioengineering has such a momentum that it continues unabated – and not always in a direction that benefits the animals involved.

What is learned through these discoveries comes from using animals under people's control. It is already possible to splice genes from one species into another. There is little doubt that within the lifespan of the youngest human generation already alive, genes that alter the behaviour, temperament and aptitudes of one species will be introduced into another. Cats will be used in these experiments because they are so readily available.

Initial genetic experiments may investigate the effect of gene splicing on benign characteristics like coat colour, coat texture and size. Once those experiments have been successfully completed, further experiments in genetic manipulation involving more complex gene sequences will take place. Scientists will be curious to see whether cat diseases can be controlled, or induced, through genetic manipulation. Remember, cats and people share perhaps eighty-five to ninety per cent of the same genes. By experimenting on cat gene sequences scientists will discover the genetic origins of human medical conditions.

By mapping gene sequences and then learning what these genes do, people will discover the very essence of life. Cats will be involved in these experiments, as will other animals such as pigs and dogs. It is an exciting and a frightening prospect. How that information will be used is a profound ethical problem all people face in the future.

INDEX